BEGINNING ROCK KEYBOARD

D1082224

Alfred, the leader in educational publishing, and the National Keyboard Workshop, one of America's finest contemporary music schools, have joined forces to bring you the best, most progressive educational tools possible. We hope you will enjoy this book and encourage you to look for other fine products from Alfred and the National Keyboard Workshop.

This book was acquired, edited and produced by Workshop Arts, Inc., the publishing arm of the National Guitar Workshop.
Nathaniel Gunod, editor
Joe Bouchard, music typesetter
Cathy Bolduc, design
CD recorded at Bar None Studios, Cheshire, CT
Cover photograph: Karen Miller

TABLE OF CONTENTS

ABOUT THE AUTHOR.................................... 4
INTRODUCTION 5

CHAPTER 1—Getting Started　6
How to Sit at the Keyboard 6
The Keyboard 7
Music Notation—Pitch 7
Ledger Lines 8
Accidentals 8
Music Notation—Time 9
Other Important Symbols 11
Half Steps, Whole Steps and the Major Scale 12
The Major Scale 12
Intervals 13

CHAPTER 2—Rock Music Theory　14
Keys, Key Signatures and Why We Use Them 14
Cycle of 5ths 15
Major Scale Fingerings 16
Minor Scales and the Relative Minor 18

CHAPTER 3—Chords　20
The Workhorse of Rock: The Triad 20
　Babylon 22
Minor Chords 23
　House of The Rising Sun 24
Major And Dominant 7th Chords 25
　First Call 26
Minor 7th Chords 27
　Isle of Dreams 27

CHAPTER 4—An Introduction to Rock Rhythms　28
Syncopation 28
Rhythm Exercises 30
Rhythmic Independence 31
　Over The Top 31
　Under The Depths 31

CHAPTER 5—Basic Bass Lines　32
　Get 'Em Up 33

CHAPTER 6—Arpeggios and Chord Inversions　34
　House of The Rising Sun: Arpeggios 35
Chord Inversions 36
Slash Chords 37
　Back To Babylon 37
Better Voice Leading Through Inversions 38
7th Chord Inversions 39
　Down To Earth 39
Pedal Tones 40
　Blue Fire 41

CHAPTER 7—Reading a Lead Sheet　42
Three Types of Lead Sheets 42
Song Form Terminology 43
Three Charts 44
　Riding On The Wind: Melody Lead Sheet 44
　Riding On The Wind: Rhythmic Notation Lead Sheet ... 45
　House Of The Rising Sun: Chord and Slash Lead Sheet.... 45

CHAPTER 8—More Left-Hand Patterns　46
Boogie-Woogie Patterns 46
　Walkin' & Talkin' 47
　This Rock'n'Roll Thing 48
Octaves 49
　Miles From Nowhere 50
　Almost There 50
Broken Octaves 51
　All Night Station 51
Boogie Lines In Octaves 52
　Saloon Spider 53

CHAPTER 9—Pentatonic Scales and Beginning Improvisation　54
Pentatonic Scales 54
　Deeper River 55
　Far As You Like 59
The Minor Pentatonic Scale 60
　New Life 61
　Off The Main Highway 62

CHAPTER 10—The Blues	63
The Blues Scale and Blue Notes	63
See The Light	64
The Grace Note	64
The Blues Shuffle or Swing Eighths	65
Roadhouse Deluxe	66
Honky Tonk Town	68
No Easy Riders	70
Diatonic Triads	71
The Twelve-Bar Blues	72
Variations on the Twelve-Bar Blues	73
Take To The Road	74
Blues Line In the Bass = Rock Power Riffs	76

CHAPTER 11—Funky Sixteenths	78
Explosive Soul	79

CHAPTER 12—In A Modal Mood	80
The Dorian Mode	81
Pure Magic	81
The Mixolydian Mode	82
Heat O' The Sun	82
Switch-A-Roo	83

CHAPTER 13—Rock Ballads	84
Roll On	84
Lady Diamond	85
Pedal Technique	86
See The Light	86

CHAPTER 14—Electronic Keyboards	88
Electric Piano	88
Lucky	88
Ping Pong	89
The Rock Organ: The Mini and the Mighty	90
Good Time Comin'	91

CHAPTER 15—More Fun Stuff: Keyboard Effects	92
Speed	92
The Gliss, or Glissando	93
Hold It Steady	93
The Tone Cluster: A Thunderous Effect!	94
Chords From Yonder	94

APPENDIX—The Major Scales	95

00
Track 1

A compact disc is available for this book. This disc can make learning with this book easier and more enjoyable. This symbol will appear next to every example that is on the CD. Use the CD to help insure that you are capturing the feel of the examples, interpreting the rhythms correctly, and so on. The track numbers below the symbols correspond directly to the example you want to hear. Track 1 will help you tune an electronic keyboard to this CD. Have fun!

ABOUT THE AUTHOR

PHOTO · BRETT VERMILYEA

Joe Bouchard is one of the founding members of the legendary rock band, Blue Öyster Cult. He joined the group in 1970 and was a creative member for sixteen years. He recorded thirteen albums with Blue Öyster Cult for Columbia Records, and was awarded nine gold albums and two platinum albums. Even though he recorded bass parts on every album, he occasionally over-dubbed keyboard parts in the studio, especially on many of the songs he wrote.

After leaving Blue Öyster Cult, Joe performed as a touring organist and pianist with Spencer Davis of the Spencer Davis Group. He has performed on stage with many top artists including J. Geils, Mike Watt, Marty Friedman of Megadeth and former Doors members, Robbie Krieger and Ray Manzarek. Joe recently released his first self-produced CD, "Solid Citizens," with his band, The X Brothers, on Cellsum Records.

Although Joe has an extensive background as a performing musician, Joe spends much of his time teaching students guitar, bass guitar and piano. He is the author of *Rock Guitar for Beginners*, published by the National Guitar Workshop and Alfred Publishing. He also hosted *Rock Bass for Beginners*, an instructional video. He holds a Bachelor of Music Education degree from Ithaca College, and a Master of Music degree from The Hartt School at the University of Hartford. Joe has taught at the National Guitar Workshop and is now an associate editor there.

ACKNOWLEDGEMENTS
Thanks to: Nat Gunod for terrific editing and guidance, Cathy Bolduc for page layout and artistic advice; Dave Smolover, Mike Allain and Paula Dutton and everyone at the National Guitar Workshop; Ron Manus, Link Harnsberger and everyone else at Alfred Publishing. Also, thanks to Collin Tilton at Bar None Studios for his great work engineering the CD and to the great musicians who played with me on the project: John Marshall (drums), Frank Brocklehurst (bass) and Mick Tino (guitar).

This project is dedicated to my family, who has always been supportive of my musical obsessions—in particular, to my mother, Frances Ryan Bouchard.

INTRODUCTION

Welcome to *Rock Keyboards for Beginners*. This book teaches everything you need to know to get started rockin' on the keys. While this book reviews all the basics, it will be helpful if you have already begun playing and reading music, at least to the level of *Alfred Basic Piano Method*, Lesson Book 2.

The use of a keyboard in rock started in the early 1950s rock'n'roll era. The hard driving piano that propelled early rock'n'roll was influenced by the blues, jazz, gospel and country styles. Rhythm and Blues (R&B), a black music style popular in many areas of the United States, combined with these other styles and gave rise to rock'n'roll.

After World War II, people in the United States needed to get up and dance, often in a loud and boisterous manner. Radio, and the proliferation of electronic instruments, made rock music accessible to everyone.

Some said it was the work of the devil, but the first rock'n'roll pianists came from the revivalist gospel churches. Jerry Lee Lewis set out to prove that the piano could be just as much a forerunner in sonic evolution as the electric guitar. Little Richard, with his flamboyant personality and hard rockin' style, played the piano with such intensity that some people must have thought that this guy was an alien from another planet. With all the joy and youthfulness of this musical style, once it got started, it just couldn't stop.

Jerry Lee Lewis had his first hit record in 1957 with the intense piano driven song, Whole Lotta Shakin' Goin' On.

Electric organs, originally designed for churches, were brought into rock music because they could be louder and were usually easier to transport than a traditional piano. Ray Manzarek of The Doors was a major champion of rock organ. Not only did he play great keyboard parts, but he also covered the bass part with his left hand, leaving great spaces for their guitarist and singer to rock hard.

Ray Manzarek's first hit record was Light My Fire *with the Doors in 1967. The album version featured an extended combo organ solo.*

The electric piano became popular late in the 1950s. This was another great texture for keyboard players to use in rock bands. The invention of the *clavinet* (a funky, synthesized harpsichord sound) came in the 1960s as rock styles evolved further into funk and soul music. In the 1970s, the evolution of the synthesizer took keyboards to the next level. Now, a rock keyboardist can create whatever their knowledge and imagination will allow. This book, like the other two books in the series, *Intermediate Rock Keyboards* and *Mastering Rock Keyboards*, is designed to help you develop YOUR

Keith Emerson is the driving force behind Emerson, Lake and Palmer, a progressive rock group founded in 1970.

knowledge and imagination. You'll learn the way rock music is made on the keyboard, learn lots of good riffs and tunes to practice, and get a solid theoretical overview to get your band rockin'!

Roll up your sleeves and let's get started.

PHOTOS OF JERRY LEE LEWIS AND RAY MANZAREK • CHUCK PULIN\COURTESY OF STARFILES, INC.
PHOTO OF KEITH EMERSON • BARRIE WENTZELL\COURTESY OF STARFILES, INC.

CHAPTER 1

Getting Started

HOW TO SIT AT THE KEYBOARD

In order to avoid physical problems, you need to understand posture and hand position.

Start on a comfortable but firm chair or bench. The height of the chair should put your elbows on the same level with the keyboard. As you depress the keys, your fingers should be slightly curved—as if holding a ball.

Rock keyboard playing gives the performer more leeway with posture than classical keyboard playing. Because rock music requires a high energy level, many keyboardists prefer to stand. Besides, a standing performer is more visible to the audience and you don't want the guitar players to hog all the glory! The biggest drawback to this approach is that it becomes more difficult to play the pedals, so you'll notice that many rock players use the pedals sparingly. If you are going to stand, raise the level of the keyboard stand so that your elbows are on the same level with the keyboard, just as in the seated position.

THE KEYBOARD

Every musical sound is represented by a *note*. On the keyboard, each note has a key that is given a letter name, A through G. After G, the sequence repeats. The keyboard, especially a full-sized one like a piano, includes many notes of the musical spectrum. You can play the bass, the chords, the melodies and all parts in between. Let's look at the basic keyboard:

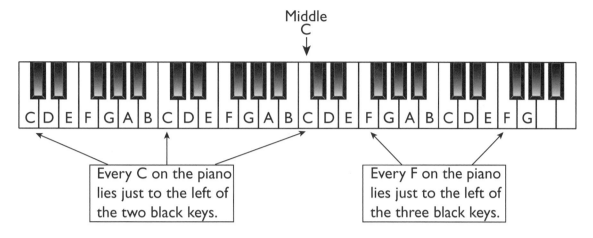

MUSIC NOTATION—PITCH

Pitch has to do with which note we play and its degree of highness or lowness. Learning to read music is largely making a mental connection between the note on the keyboard and the notes on the page. We write music on five lines and four spaces. It is easy if we see the horizontal lines as a big grid that tells us how high (toward the right side of the keyboard) or how low (toward the left side) the notes are from the center. That grid of five lines and four spaces is called the *staff*. In keyboard music, two staves are often connected in a *grand staff*—one staff for each hand.

Compare the notes on this grand staff to the keyboard diagram above.

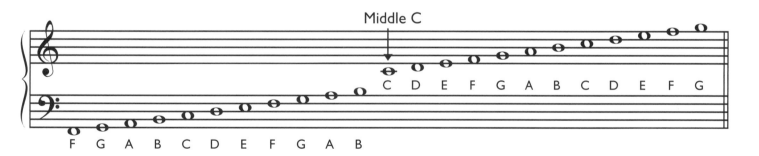

At the beginning of each staff there is a symbol called a *clef*. The *treble clef* 𝄞 is for the high pitched notes, usually played with the right hand (R.H.). Its curly end surrounds the "G" line. For this reason, it is sometimes called the *G clef*.

The *bass clef* 𝄢 is for the lower pitched notes played in the left hand (L.H.). The two dots surround the "F" line. For this reason, it is sometimes called the *F clef*.

Clefs designate the relative highness or lowness of the tones and help keep the notes organized on the lines. As you become more familiar with these symbols, recognizing the names of the notes will become much easier.

LEDGER LINES

We use ledger lines to write notes that are higher or lower than those that fit on the staff. They are short lines that extend the staff either higher or lower. We can use just about any number of ledger lines to write very high or very low notes, but the more ledger lines there are, the harder it is to read the notes at a glance. Ledger lines become easy to read with experience. If you must, count the lines up or down by letter names until you find the name of the note, then mark it with a pencil. This will help you memorize the ledger line names.

MIDDLE C

Middle C is a major "landmark" on the keyboard. If you know where it is, you'll never be completely lost. It sits on a ledger line between the treble and bass staves.

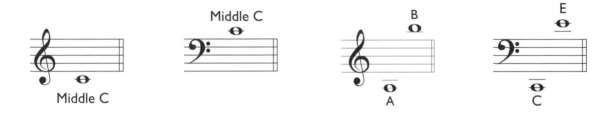

ACCIDENTALS

The black keys on the keyboard are called *accidentals*. They can either have a *sharp* name ♯ or a *flat* name ♭. The letter name is determined by the adjacent note. When the normal note (white key) is raised one key to the right (higher in pitch), we use the sharp name. When the normal note is moved one key to the left (lower in pitch), we use the flat name. For example, the black note to the right of D is D♯. The black note to the left of E is E♭. They both use the same black key! Notes that sound the same but have different names are called *enharmonic* notes.

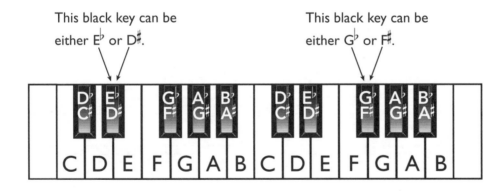

When a note is made sharp or flat, it stays that way until something happens to make it natural again. One important way notes are returned to their natural position is with a natural sign ♮.

This is what accidentals look like on the staff.

 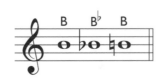  

NOTE AND REST VALUES

Pitches must be played in a framework of time to make the music come to life. A system of note values and *rest* (silence) values have been developed over the centuries to show the player how long to play a note or how long to be silent.

The basic unit of time in music is a *beat*. Each note is held for a specific amount of time that is measured in beats. For example, a *quarter note* ♩ usually lasts for one beat (see the section on time signatures, below). Beats are the basic pulse behind music. Here is a chart of the basic note values:

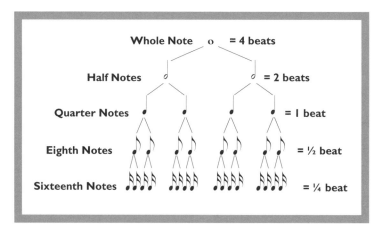

Rest values have the same structure as note values:

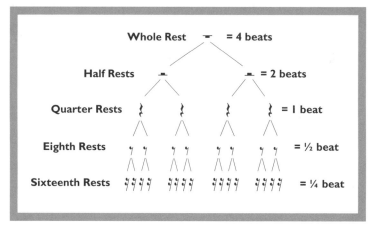

MEASURES AND BAR LINES

The staff is divided by vertical lines called *bar lines*. The space between two bar lines is called a *measure*. Measures (sometimes called *bars*) divide music into groups of beats. A *double bar* marks the end of a section or example. The *final bar* signals the end of the piece of music.

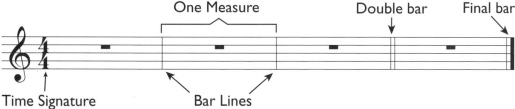

Time Signature   Bar Lines

TIME SIGNATURE

Each piece begins with a *time signature*. The numbers in a time signature tell us how to count time in the musical piece or song. The bottom number shows the kind of note that equals one beat (4 indicates a quarter note; 8 indicates an eighth note, etc.). The top number shows how many beats are in each measure.

4 = Four beats per measure
4 = The quarter note ♩ = one beat

6 = Six beats per measure
8 = The eighth note ♪ = one beat

BEAMS

Some of the notes on the previous page were designated with flags on their stems.

Beamed eighth notes

We can connect the stems with fat lines called *beams* in order to keep them neater on the page and, hence, easier to read when seen in a group. Here are examples of *beamed notes*.

1 & 2 & 3 & 4 &

Beamed sixteenth notes

1 e & ah 2 e & ah

TIES

A note or rest value can be increased by use of a tie. A tie is made with a curved line called a *slur* that connects two or more notes. You would play the first note and hold that note through the time value of the second, tied note. In other words, do not strike the tied note—just continue to hold the first note for the tied note's value. On the right are some tied notes. Notice the counting numbers below the staff. Don't sound the notes that fall over the counting numbers in parentheses.

Notes can be tied over bar lines, as in this example.

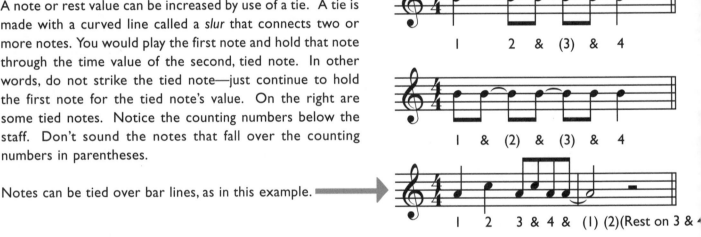

1   2 & (3) & 4

1 & (2) & (3) & 4

1   2   3 & 4 & (1) (2)(Rest on 3 &

DOTS

The dot is a handy add-on to a note. It increases the value of the note by half of its given value. For example, a half note (two beats) with a dot would increase in value by one beat (a dotted-half note equals three beats). Here are some dotted notes:

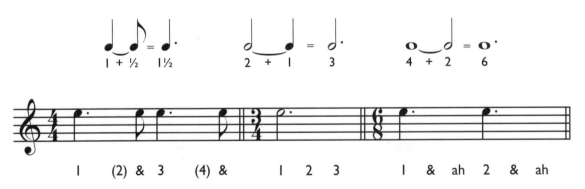

1 + ½   1½   2 + 1   3   4 + 2   6

1   (2) & 3   (4) &   1   2   3   1 & ah 2 & ah

Notice that in $\frac{6}{8}$, the six eighth notes can be divided into two beats, each containing three eighth notes. Instead of counting 1-2-3-4-5-6, count 1 & ah, 2 & ah. So, we can say that in $\frac{6}{8}$, the dotted-quarter note (equal to three eighth notes) equals one beat. There are then two beats per measure!

TRIPLETS

A *triplet* is a group of three notes played in the time of two notes with the same value. For example, two regular eighth notes divide a beat into equal parts. An eighth-note triplet divides a beat into three equal parts.

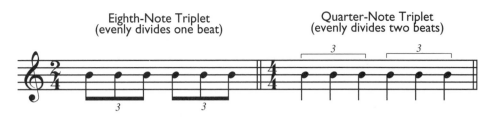

Eighth-Note Triplet
(evenly divides one beat)

Quarter-Note Triplet
(evenly divides two beats)

OTHER IMPORTANT SYMBOLS

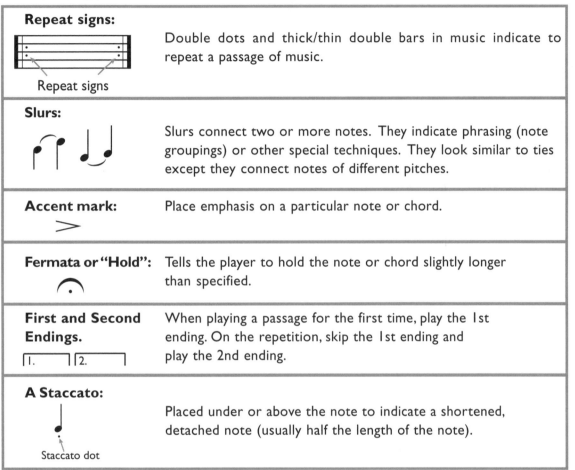

Repeat signs: Repeat signs	Double dots and thick/thin double bars in music indicate to repeat a passage of music.
Slurs:	Slurs connect two or more notes. They indicate phrasing (note groupings) or other special techniques. They look similar to ties except they connect notes of different pitches.
Accent mark:	Place emphasis on a particular note or chord.
Fermata or "Hold":	Tells the player to hold the note or chord slightly longer than specified.
First and Second Endings. 1. 2.	When playing a passage for the first time, play the 1st ending. On the repetition, skip the 1st ending and play the 2nd ending.
A Staccato: Staccato dot	Placed under or above the note to indicate a shortened, detached note (usually half the length of the note).

FINGERING

Playing the keyboard smoothly often requires that you use specific fingers in a specific order. Fingerings for the right hand are placed above the notes. Fingerings for the left hand are placed below the notes. Here are the numbers of the fingers, the thumb being "1" for both hands, the index finger "2" for both hands, etc.

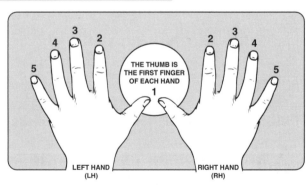

TIP

You should practice with a metronome, drum box or click to keep the *tempo* (the relative speed of the music) steady. Keeping a solid beat is very important, especially in a rock band.

At the beginning of each example you will find a metronome marking like this: ♩ = 72

This means the quarter note, or one beat, will proceed at a tempo of 72 beats per minute. While you can play the examples faster or slower than the marked tempo, it will give you a point of departure. It is a good idea to start practicing much slower, and work up to the recommended tempo.

Understanding the keyboard is made easy with a system of measuring the distance between two or more notes. These distances are called *intervals*. The most basic of these are *half steps* and *whole steps*.

The diagrams below show how these intervals relate to the keyboard.

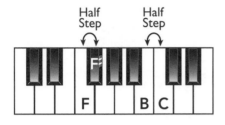

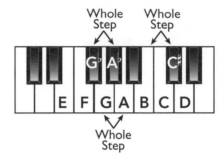

THE MAJOR SCALE

A *scale* is a group of notes organized in alphabetical order. Scales are the building blocks of harmony and melody. Every type of scale is organized with a specific arrangement of half steps and whole steps. The most important scale by far is the major scale. The diagram below shows a major scale starting on C, the C Major scale, and the formula of half steps and whole steps.

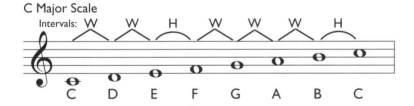

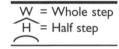

This formula of ontervals will create a major scale no matter which note is the starting note, or *root*. However, starting on any note other than C will necessitate the use of accidentals. You will find it necessary to use either sharps or flats, but never both! The note names must always progress in alphabetical order. Here is a D Major scale. Notice that to create the whole step between the 2nd and 3rd degrees, you must use an F♯. The same situation arises between the 6th and 7th degrees. Check it out:

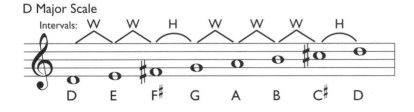

INTERVALS

All the notes of a major scale are given *scale degree* numbers based on their distance from the root. They are all given *quality* names: either *major* or *perfect*. In this system, a whole step up from the root of the scale is called a *major 2nd*. In fact, any whole step is called a major 2nd. Here are the major and perfect intervals in relation to the root of a C Major scale. The numbers below show the distance measured in half steps.

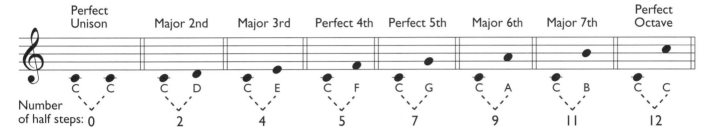

When the notes are altered with an accidental, or are an interval (distance) not found above the root of the major scale, they are given other quality names: *minor, diminished* and *augmented*. Notice that the interval of a half step is now called a *minor 2nd*.

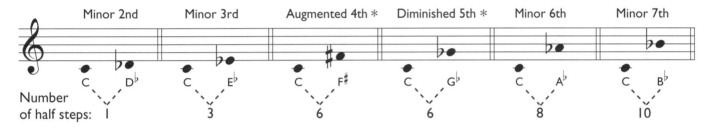

As you construct chords and other scales later in the book, these concepts become very important.

Refer to the chart below to learn the numbers and interval names based on size in half steps.

CHART OF INTERVALS

Number	Number of Half Steps	Interval	Abbreviation
1	0	perfect unison	PU
♭2	1	minor 2nd	min2
2	2	major 2nd	Maj2
♭3	3	minor 3rd	min3
3	4	major 3rd	Maj3
4	5	perfect 4th	P4
♯4 *	6 ("tritone")	augmented 4th	Aug4
♭5 *	6	diminished 5th	dim5
5	7	perfect 5th	P5
♯5	8	augmented 5th	Aug5
♭6	8	minor 6th	min6
6	9	major 6th	Maj6
♭7	10	minor 7th	min7
7	11	major 7th	Maj7
1	12	perfect octave	P8

* The augmented 4th and diminished 5th intervals are enharmonically the same and sometimes called a tritone.

Exercise:

Try forming each of these intervals going both up and down from different notes on the keyboard. Play them both *melodically* (one note at a time) and *harmonically* (both notes at the same time).

CHAPTER 2

Rock Music Theory

KEYS, KEY SIGNATURES AND WHY WE USE THEM

Each rock tune revolves around a specific pitch we call the *tonal center*. That pitch is the *root* of the *key*. The root, or *key note*, will be the root of the scale that is used to create the song. If a C Major scale was used, then we are *in the key of C*. Even in a simple song, the music may stray away from the key, but it usually comes back to a satisfying ending or, to use baseball terminology, "home plate."

This is where the *key signature* comes in. A key signature is a group of sharps or flats shown at the beginning of a line of music. It is comprised of either sharps or flats, never a combination. The sharps or flats in a key signature are derived from the major scale. The key signature for D Major will include F♯ and C♯ because those are the accidentals that occur when we build a major scale starting on D. By checking the chart on page 15, we can count the number of sharps or flats for each key.

Since there are no sharps or flats in the C Major scale, there is nothing in the key signature for the key of C. The example below is in the key of C. Play the melody and listen to its sound.

The chart on page 15 shows all the key signatures. The sharp and flat signs sit on the line or space they affect. For example, a flat on the B line represents B♭. This tells us that every B in the tune is played B♭ unless otherwise indicated with a natural sign. This is a great type of shorthand…it saves writing out all those accidentals! It also tells us in a heartbeat that the key is F, because only the F Major scale has just a B♭. Study the key signature chart. Over time, you will need to memorize the key signatures.

THE KEY SIGNATURES

It should be noted that there is a key of F#, but since it uses the same notes as G♭, we will only use G♭ for now.

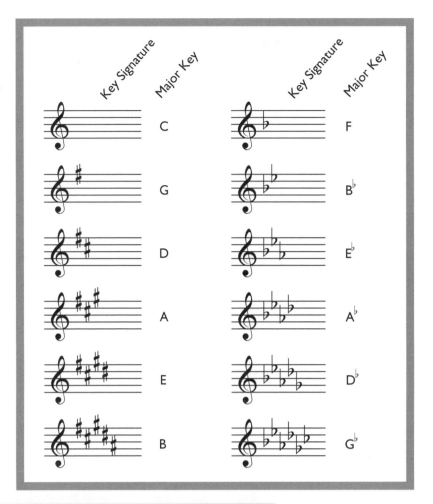

CYCLE OF 5THS

The *cycle of 5ths* (also known as the *circle of 5ths*) helps us understand how keys relate to each other. Often, songs can shift keys in midstream. Knowing how the keys relate, and which accidentals to look out for, is important. Notice that if you go clockwise around the circle, or up by 5ths, a sharp is added to each key: G has one sharp, D has two, A has three, etc. If you go counter-clockwise around the circle, up by 4ths (or down by 5ths—it's the same thing), a flat is added to each key: F has one flat, B♭ has two, etc.

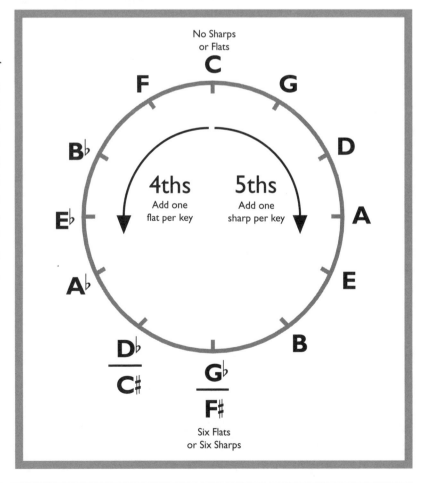

A *fingering* is a specific order of fingers to use in a tune or scale. Learning any major scale fingering will help you get comfortable with its key. Playing scales is also a great exercise for building up your keyboard technique.

Here is the right-hand fingering for the C Major scale:

*Notice that the 4th is played by crossing your thumb underneath fingers 2 and 3. This positions you to finish the scale using the fingers in order, 1, 2, 3, 4 and 5. Since there are eight notes in the scale, and you only have five fingers, you'll always have to cross the fingers.

In the left hand fingerings, it's done differently. The 3rd finger crosses over 1 to play the 6th.

Practice the right and left hands hand separately. When you've mastered both, play them together.

C Major Scale

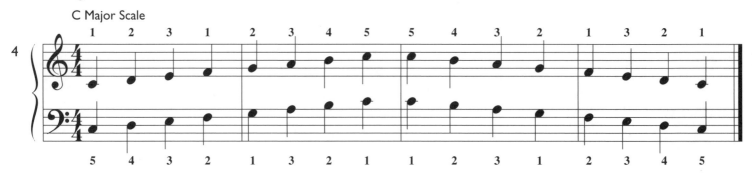

Here is the G Major scale. As with the C Major scale, practice both hands separately before putting them together.

G Major Scale

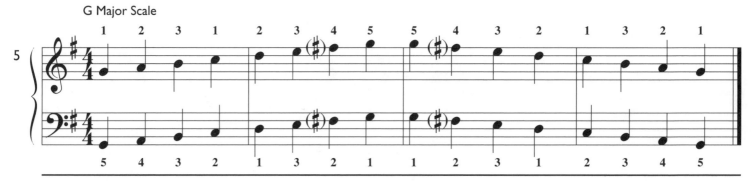

Here are major scale fingerings for some common rock keys. See the appendix on page 95
for all the major scales with fingerings.

D MAJOR SCALE

A MAJOR SCALE

The patterns are different for the next two.

F MAJOR SCALE

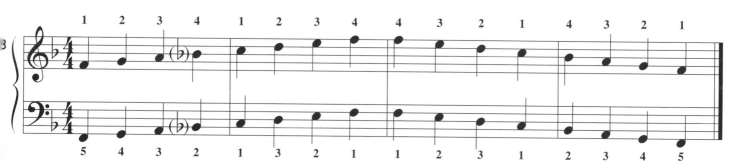

B♭ MAJOR SCALE

Minor keys have a distinctively darker, sadder and possibly more intense sound than major keys. All minor scales are closely related to a major scale. The 6th degree of any major scale is the root of a minor scale. For example, if you count up to the 6th degree of a C Major scale, you'll arrive at "A." Now, if you play the notes of the C Major scale, but start and end on "A," you will have played the A *Natural Minor* scale. This kind of minor scale is called "natural minor" because the notes of its relative major scale (the scale it was derived from) are left unchanged.

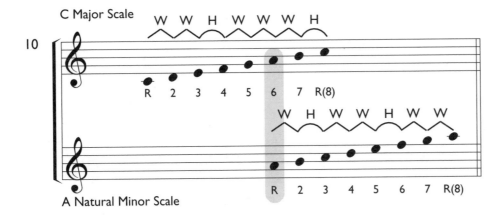

R = Root

The key of A Minor is the *relative minor key* to C Major. Every major key has its corresponding minor key.

MAJOR KEY	RELATIVE MINOR
G	E
D	B
A	F#
E	C#
B	G#
F	D
B♭	G
E♭	C
A♭	F
D♭	B♭
G♭	E♭

Here are several natural minor scales and their fingerings.

A NATURAL MINOR

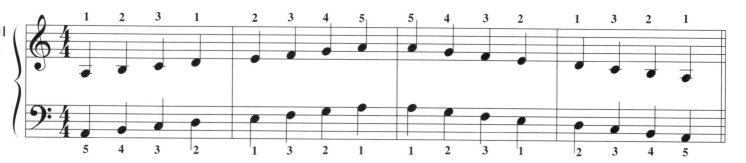

E NATURAL MINOR

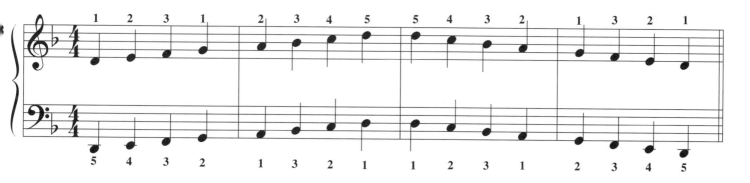

D NATURAL MINOR

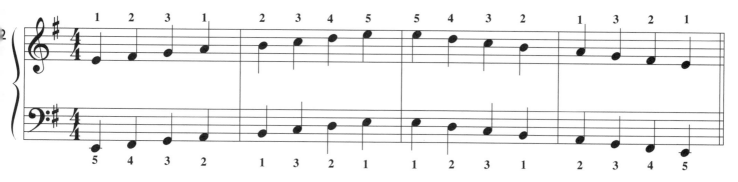

G NATURAL MINOR

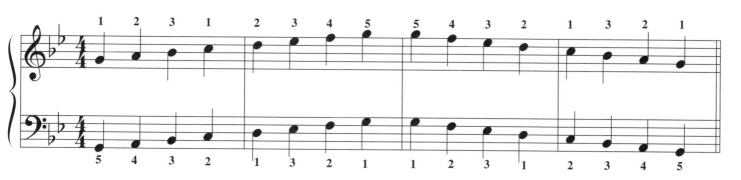

CHAPTER 3

Chords

THE WORKHORSE OF ROCK: THE TRIAD

A *chord* is a group of three or more notes played together. A *triad* is a three-note chord. Most rock music uses triads. Triads are derived from the major scale, and are built with intervals of a 3rd. For example, if you play the root, 3rd and 5th of a C Major scale, you will create the C Major triad. It's that easy!

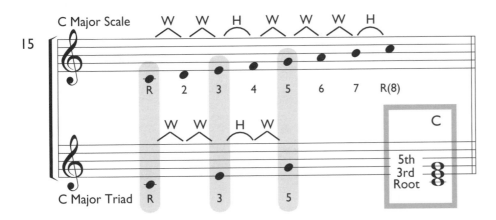

Let's check the intervals used in the C Major triad (in rock lingo, we would simply say "C chord").

All major triads have the same formula of interval relationships:

> **1 = The Root.**
> **3 = The middle note or 3rd of the chord (a major 3rd above the root).**
> **5 = The upper note or 5th of the chord (a minor 3rd above the 3rd**
>   **or**
>   **a perfect 5th above the root).**

We built our C chord on the root of a C Major scale. We can build similar triads on the root of any major scale. Let's build a few more chords. Notice how all major chords have the same formula.

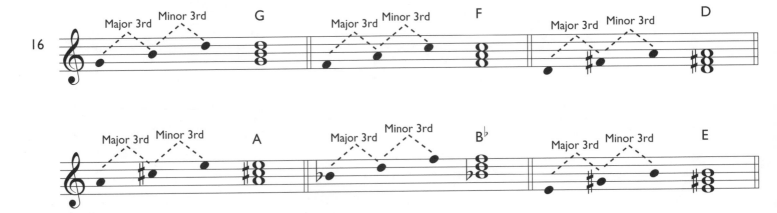

Here is a good exercise for learning the major chords. Learn it with your right hand and then with the left. The chord names are written above the music. Notice that chords with sharps in their names can also be called by their flat names. For example, C♯ can also be called D♭, A♯ can also be called B♭, and so on.

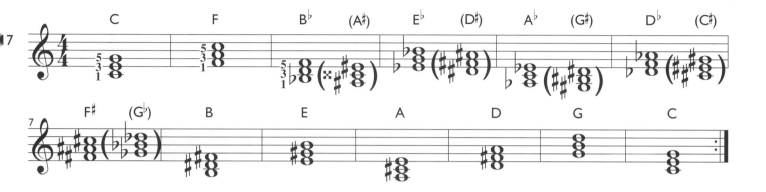

Here are the same chords played with the left hand.

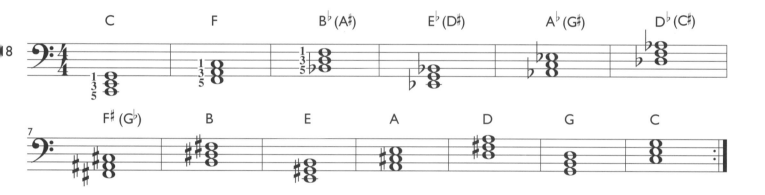

Booker T. Jones *was the leader of* Booker T. and the MGs *who scored a major hit with* Green Onions *in 1962. They were responsible for creating the "Memphis Sound" and played on most of the big hits for Stax Records.*

Here is a tune that uses major chords. The right hand plays mostly eighth-note triads and the left hand plays single notes. Follow the counting under the treble clef staff.

Practice Tip:

Don't forget the repeat sign in bar 8. Go back to the beginning and play the first eight measures again. Then, continue to the end. Also, there is a fermata (see page 11) on the last chord.

mf = *Mezzoforte. Moderately loud.*

BABYLON
Track 3

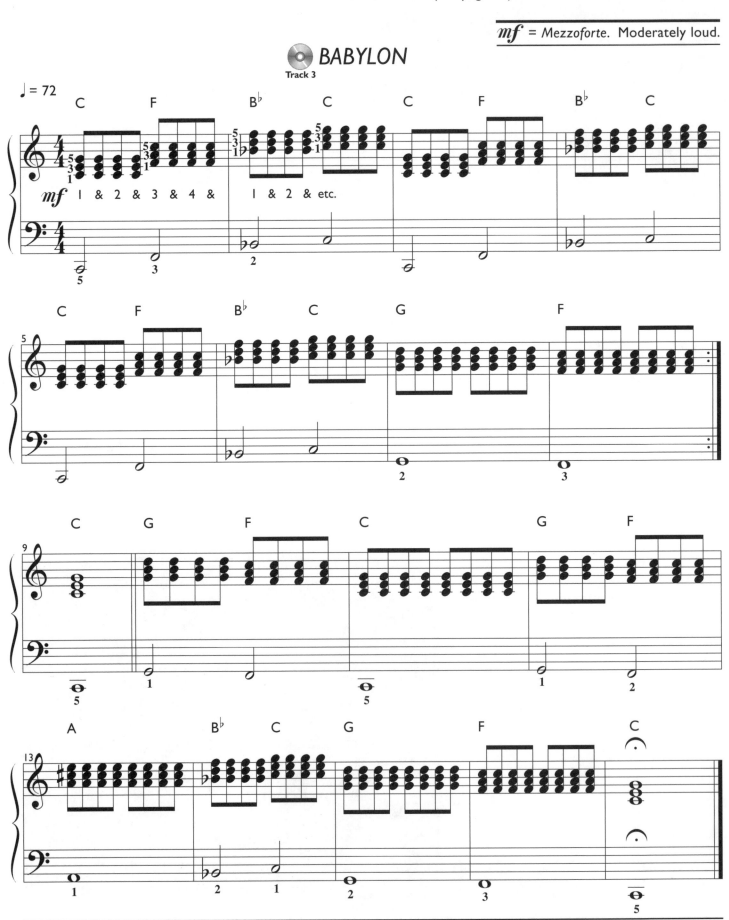

Like major chords, minor chords are derived from scales. The formula for a minor triad is:

1 = The Root.
♭3 = The middle note or flat 3rd of the chord (a minor 3rd above the root).
5 = The upper note or 5th of the chord (a major 3rd above the flat 3rd
or
a perfect 5th above the root).

The example below shows how a minor triad can be derived from the 1st, 3rd and 5th degrees of a minor scale.

A Natural Minor Scale

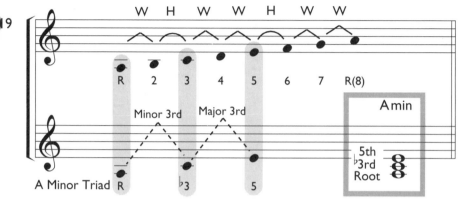

Below is an example comparing a C Major chord with a C Minor. Notice how the major triad can be made minor by lowering the 3rd. In sheet music, this chord is known as Cmin or Cm.

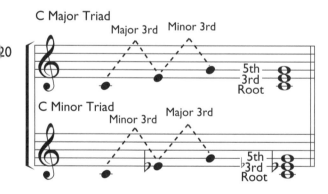

Here is an exercise to help you get acquainted with minor chords. Notice that the chords are ordered in a cycle of 4ths (descending cycle of 5ths).

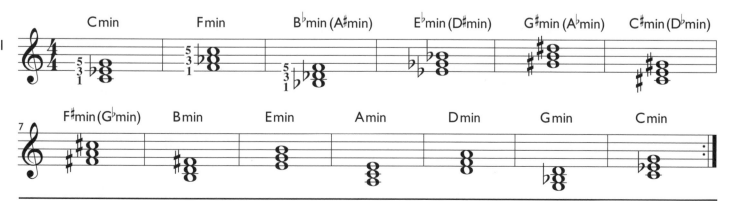

House of the Rising Sun is a traditional tune in the key of A Minor. Notice that it includes the A Minor chord. Eric Burden and the Animals recorded this song in the 1960s and it became an instant rock classic. Their arrangement featured a great rock keyboard part. In the arrangement provided here, the first section has the vocal melody in the right hand. The second section has chords in the right hand and a single-note bass line in the left.

This tune uses the $\frac{12}{8}$ time signature. There are twelve beats in each measure but we think of them in groups of three, with 1, 4, 7 and 10 being the "strong" beats (slightly accented). The result is really four beats per measure with each beat divided into three eighth notes (count 1-&-ah, 2-&-ah, etc.). This is called a *compound meter*. Four beats per measure with each beat divided into two eighth notes, $\frac{4}{4}$, is called a *simple meter*.

Here is how the rhythm to this song is counted:

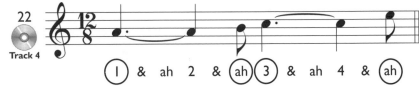

The first note in this tune is a *pickup note*, which is a note that occurs before the first full measure. This one comes on the "ah" after beat "4." This incomplete measure is always balanced by an incomplete measure at the end.

$\boldsymbol{f}$ = Forte. Loud

HOUSE OF THE RISING SUN

MAJOR AND DOMINANT 7TH CHORDS

Most early rock tunes use simple major and minor triads. But occasionally rock players will use 7th chords to really make the tunes "sizzle"! A 7th chord is a four-note chord. If you take a triad and add a tone a 7th up from the root, you have a 7th chord. You can also think of it as adding another 3rd above the 5th of a triad.

Let's look at a C Major triad with a 7th added above the 5th.

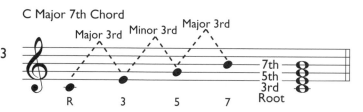

In sheet music, this chord is known as **CMaj7 or CM7.**

Example 23 demonstrates that if you use the 7th that occurs naturally in the major scale of the root of the chord (in this case, the C Major scale), the 7th is a major 7th, forming a *major 7th chord*. The major 7th chord is an excellent, sweet-sounding chord. Once in a while we sneak it into rock tunes. Red Hot Chili Peppers use a major 7th in *Under The Bridge* with great effectiveness.

In rock, the bluesy sounding *dominant 7th chord* is more commonly used. This kind of 7th chord has a ♭7 or minor 7th—the 7th is lowered one half step. Example 24 shows the formula for this cool sounding chord. Play it loud. Dominant 7th chords rock!

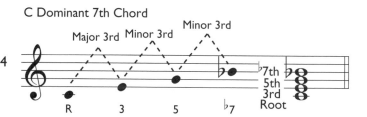

In sheet music, this chord is known as **C7.**

This exercise will give you some practice with dominant 7th chords. After you play it with the right hand, play it an octave lower with the left.

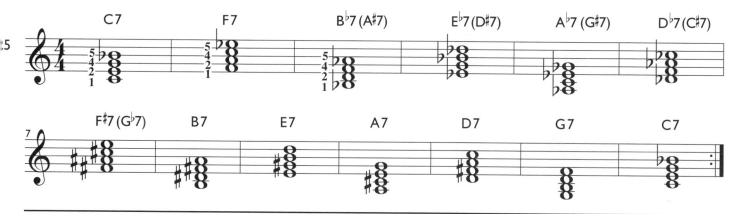

Let's play a tune using dominant 7th chords.

FIRST CALL

Track 6

(*Last time only)

Steve Winwood became famous in 1967 as the singer and keyboard player for the Spencer Davis Group. He later formed the group Traffic and became a very successful solo artist in the 1980s and 1990s.

Just as we add a ♭7 to a major chord to create a dominant 7th chord, we can add a ♭7 to a minor chord to create the four-note minor 7th chord. The example below shows the formula for a minor 7th chord.

C Minor 7th Chord

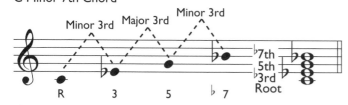

In sheet music, this chord is known as **Cmin7 or Cm7.**

This exercise will give you some practice with minor 7th chords. After you play it with the right hand, play it an octave lower with the left.

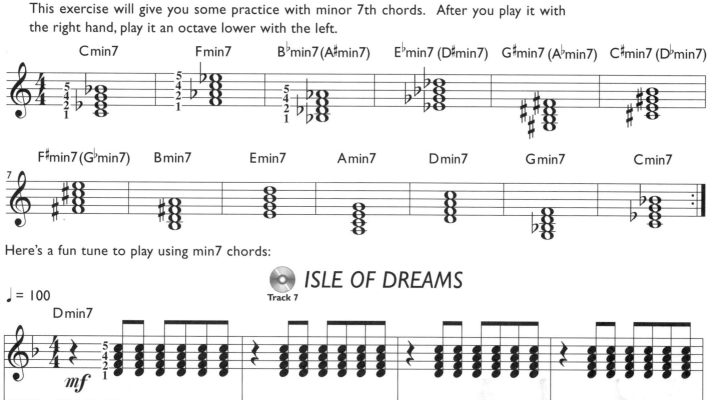

Here's a fun tune to play using min7 chords:

ISLE OF DREAMS
Track 7

CHAPTER 4

An Introduction to Rock Rhythms

The success of a good rock tune has a lot to do with strong rhythms. It doesn't take long to understand this concept if you hear a great live rock band pumping the music along at full tilt. The best of the bunch always have tremendous rhythms.

This style of music grew up in a time where unschooled or minimally trained musicians liberally borrowed the best rhythmic ideas from jazz, early blues and boogie-woogie. Boogie's repetitive bass lines were tossed into a stew with a dash of country simplicity making a rhythmic dish that became known as rock'n'roll. By pointing this musical feel at the emotions of the teens of the 1950s and '60s it became, and still is, one of the most popular musical styles ever.

You MUST get that rhythm thing happening to make it ROCK!

This is usually hashed out in the garages, rehearsal rooms and dance halls by bands trying to emulate their rock'n'roll heroes. But here are two secrets:

#1. Make sure the time, or pulse, of the music is as steady as a ticking clock. Play along with your favorite recordings or use a metronome or similar device.

#2. Make sure everyone in your band feels the rhythm together. Listen carefully as you play.

SYNCOPATION

Often, the difficulty in reading rhythms lies in the fact that music on the printed page *looks* harder than it actually is to play. This is because of *syncopation*. Syncopation is a shifting of the accent to a weak beat or weak part of a beat. In $\frac{4}{4}$ time, beats 1 and 3 are strong beats; beats 2 and 4 are weak. The *off-beats*—the "&s"—are the weak parts of the beats. The *on-beats*—where we count the numbers (1, 2, 3, 4)—are the strong parts of the beats.

To understand the concepts of off-beats and on-beats, you should study your feet. If you stomp your feet to the beat of a song with a steady rhythm, you learn that there are on-beats (when your foot is firmly planted on the floor) and off-beats (when your foot is lifted off the floor).

Here is a diagram of feet doing what they do to good rock music.

TAPPING YOUR FEET

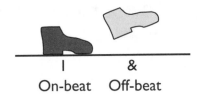

On-beat   Off-beat

In example 28, play a note on each on-beat. Keep the beat very steady.

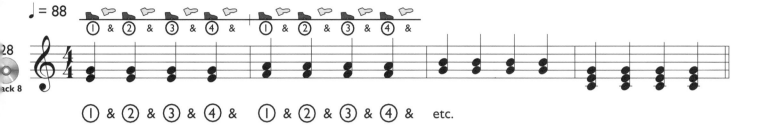

① & ② & ③ & ④ &   ① & ② & ③ & ④ &   etc.

Good! But after awhile, rhythm like this can sound stiff. You may need more of that rock'n'roll, rhythmic punch.

> = *Accent.* Play the note or chord louder.

Try example 29. It includes a syncopation. The second accent is moved half a beat to the right of the second beat. The accents fall on beat 1 and the "&" of 2.

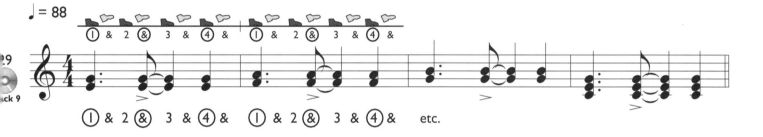

① & 2 ② 3 & ④ &   ① & 2 ② 3 & ④ &   etc.

Use your metronome or drum machine. This will help you keep a steady tempo and make it easy to find the on-beats.

This seems simple enough. But syncopation often looks difficult on the printed page because it is frequently accomplished with ties. We read two notes when only one is sounded. If you write the beats under the music, it will be easier. As in the examples printed on this page, write the numbers with their "&" symbols (1 & 2 & 3 & 4 &). This will help you determine if you should play on a downbeat (1, 2, 3, 4) or an up-beat ("&"). You'll be rockin' in no time at all!

Here is another syncopated example using ties:

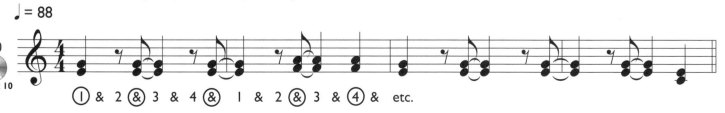

① & 2 ② 3 & 4 ④   1 & 2 ② 3 & ④ &   etc.

This example is in the style of Bo Diddley, a master of syncopated rhythms.

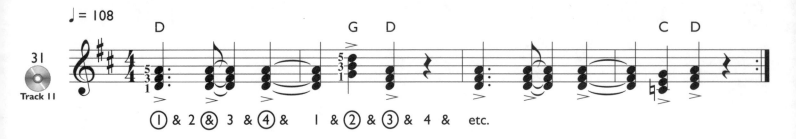

Example 32 uses dotted notes and ties over the bar line to create syncopations. Make sure the last F chord comes on beat 3. Avoid the tendency to lose track of the on-beat when playing lots of off-beats.

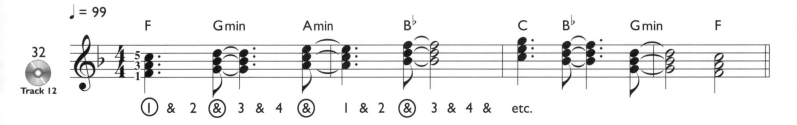

Let's combine a straight quarter-note rhythm in the left hand with syncopations in the right hand. Be careful to keep the left hand steady as you play the accents in the right hand. One of the most important things to learn when playing keyboards is independence between the hands. This will be addressed in detail on page 31.

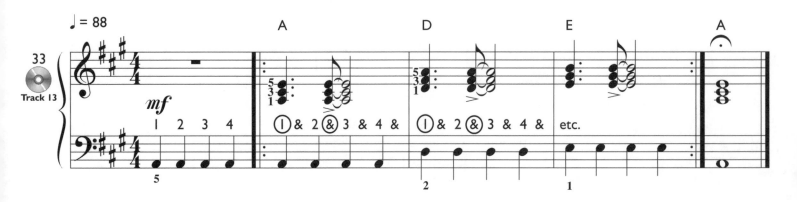

RHYTHMIC INDEPENDENCE

One of the important things a keyboardist must master is the ability to play two different rhythms simultaneously, one in the left hand and one in the right. Practice each tune very slowly, one hand at a time. Then, put the hands together, also very slowly, until each hand feels independent of the other. Finally, try a faster pace.

OVER THE TOP
Track 14

This exercise has syncopations in the right hand and steady eighth notes in the left.

UNDER THE DEPTHS
Track 15

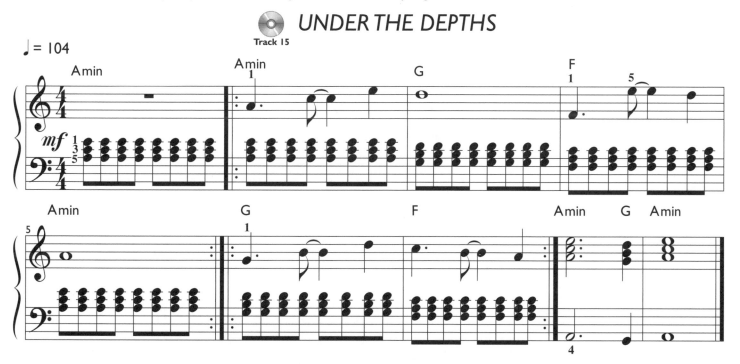

After a bit of practice, the concept of syncopation starts to settle into the familiar. The trick is not to panic when you see the dots and ties, but to work things out with some simple counting. Always include the "&" in your counting. This is called subdividing. Use a pencil and mark the on-beats and off-beats in the music.

This chapter has been an introduction to syncopations using eighth notes. On page 78, we will look at syncopations using sixteenth notes, the kind that funk players build their songs around.

CHAPTER 5

Basic Bass Lines

It's the night of the big gig. You're on the bandstand, ready to rock out with your killer keyboard parts. Suddenly the band leader turns to you and says:

"Bad news…the bass player's car broke down. He's stuck in the breakdown lane of the Jersey Turnpike. He's not gonna make it tonight. Your left hand is the bass player now. Good luck!"

At this point, you either break into a cold sweat and run out of the room screaming, or you open your massive mental file of cool bass lines and say, "Let's rock!"

Rock music always has strong bass lines. In the early days of rock'n'roll, pianists like Jerry Lee Lewis and Fats Domino played hard rockin' left-hand bass lines—often borrowed from barrelhouse or boogie-woogie piano—that vigorously drove the music forward.

A rock keyboardist might be called upon to double the bass guitar part for an even more solid bottom-end sound. The Doors, the legendary 1960s act led by Jim Morrison, never had a bass player in concert. Ray Manzarek's left hand on a Fender keyboard bass provided their bass. As the scenario above suggests, you may have to play bass on a synthesizer or keyboard sampler someday, so let's learn some left-hand patterns.

The simplest left-hand part might be just holding the left hand in whole or half notes while the right hand plays the chords (see *Babylon* on page 22). It's more likely, however, that you'll need to lay down some rockin' rhythms. Here are a few classic patterns. Count carefully to master the syncopated rhythms.

Let's put some of those patterns together in a song.

GET 'EM UP

CHAPTER 6

Arpeggios and Chord Inversions

Arpeggios are broken chords. On the keyboard, this is a simple matter of playing chords in varying patterns, up and down, mostly one note at a time.

Here are some common arpeggio patterns. Play these with the right hand and then an octave lower with the left hand.

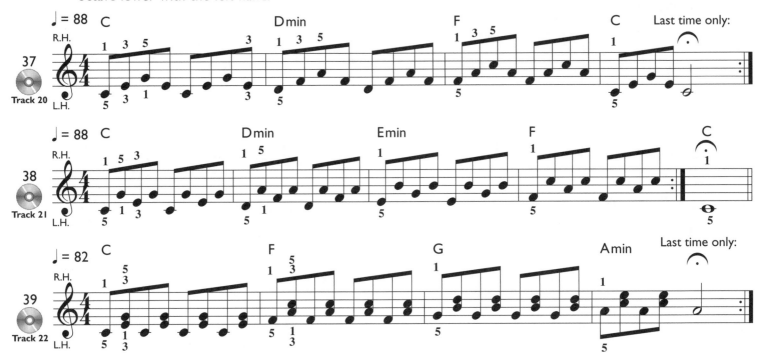

Notice that the next example is written in bass clef, for the left hand. Also play it an octave higher with the right hand.

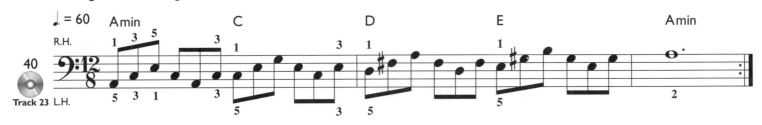

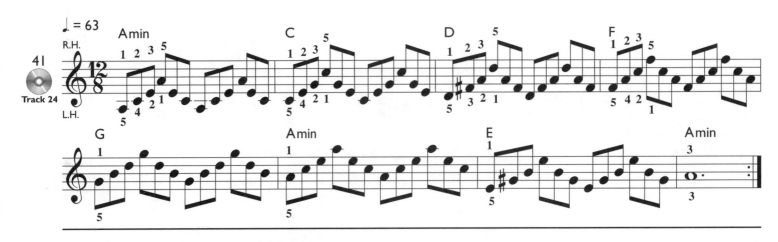

You first learned *House of the Rising Sun* on page 24. Here's your old friend back again, this time as an *accompaniment*, or backing part, with arpeggios.

HOUSE OF THE RISING SUN: ARPEGGIOS

Track 25

Billy Preston *is a brilliant keyboardist who became a unofficial member of the Beatles in 1969, performing with them on their "Let It Be" album. In the 1970s, he became a very successful solo artist and had several hit records. He continues to perform with artists such as Ringo Starr and the Rolling Stones.*

CHORD INVERSIONS

So far in this book, we've played all our chords in *root position*. In other words, the root is the lowest note of the chord. But chords are often *inverted*. When a chord is inverted, something other than the root is the lowest note.

If the 3rd of the chord is on the bottom, it is said to be in *1st inversion*.
If the 5th of that chord is on the bottom, it is said to be in *2nd inversion*.

We have good reasons for using inversions:

1) To make the chord easier to finger and make smoother changes from one chord to another.
2) To make the chord sound higher or lower without going into the next octave.
3) To make smooth bass lines.

Here are four different major chords and their inversions:

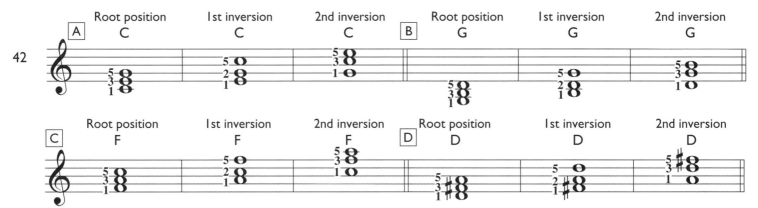

Minor chords are inverted in exactly the same way. Here are two different minor chords and their inversions:

The lowest note of the chord always determines the inversion, even if the lowest note is in the left hand. We can play an inversion with the right hand, but it is not truly an inversion if the left hand is playing the root. Below are a few inversions for both hands. Notice that a triad can be spread out so that the three notes are split up between the hands. Furthermore, it is important to note that the left hand is often doubling a note that is also being played in the right hand. Virtually any combination of the chord tones is possible, although some may be more desirable than others. In the end, your ear will be your guide. This important aspect of music is called *voicing*.

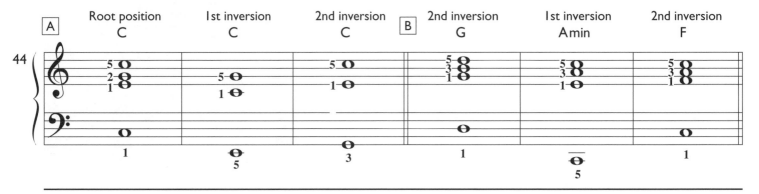

In rock music, you will often see chord symbols with a slash (C/G, Dmin/C, F/D, etc.). A slash chord tells you there is an inversion lurking about. For instance, C/E tells you there is a 1st inversion C chord. C is the chord name and the lowest note is an E. The E is the 3rd of the chord.

Slash chords can aid in building totally different and interesting harmonies. For instance, C/D is a C chord with a D in the bass. The D is not a chord tone, so it makes for an interesting, colorful chord. You'll learn about cool *chord extensions* such as this in *Intermediate Rock Keyboard*.

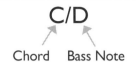

In slash chords, the letter before the slash is the chord and the letter after the slash is the bass note.

C/D

Chord   Bass Note

You will find that many inversions feel easier to play than the same chord in root position. Here is a tune you learned on page 22 but arranged here to include inverted chords.

mp = Moderately soft

BACK TO BABYLON
Track 26

BETTER VOICE LEADING THROUGH INVERSIONS

Below are two versions of the same chord pattern. The first version uses all root position chords in the right hand. The second version uses mostly inverted chords in the right hand. The left-hand part is identical in both. It is possible that one might prefer the first version in some cases, but the second version is easier to play and smoother sounding. Each note of each chord moves more smoothly to each note of the next chord. This is a great example of using inversions to create better *voice leading*.

ALL ROOT POSITION CHORDS

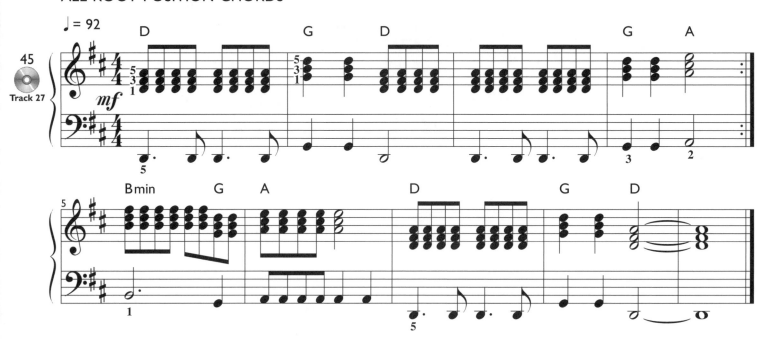

WITH INVERSIONS FOR BETTER VOICE LEADING

7TH CHORD INVERSIONS

Just as major and minor triads can be inverted, four-note 7th chords can be inverted. The difference is that since they have four notes, they can be inverted three times. The *3rd inversion* has the 7th as the lowest note of the chord.

Here are four different 7th chords with all three of their inversions. Notice how slash chords are used to indicate chord inversions.

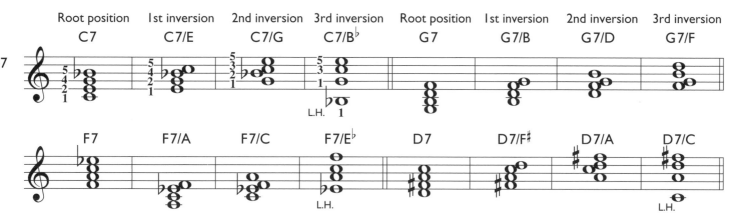

The same concept can be applied to minor 7th chords. Try lowering the 3rd of each 7th chord in example 47 to create minor 7th chord inversions.

Down to Earth uses 7th chord inversions. Enjoy the rich sound of the chords. Notice the smooth, step-wise movement of the bass. This is a great reason for using inversions. Have fun!

DOWN TO EARTH
Track 29

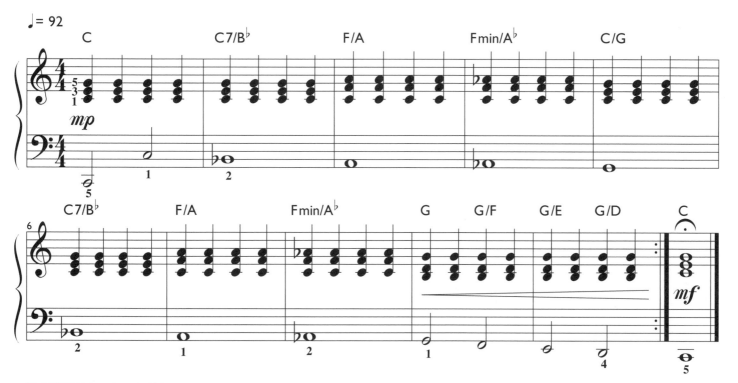

It is a common rock technique to change chords in the right hand while holding a single, unchanging note in the left hand. As the chords change, *dissonance* (a clashing sound) occurs causing tension and, often, suspense. The unchanging note in the left hand is called a *pedal tone*. The term "pedal tone" is taken from an organ technique wherein the performer holds down a floor-pedal note with a foot, while playing a series of chords with the hands above the held note.

The following examples use pedal tones.

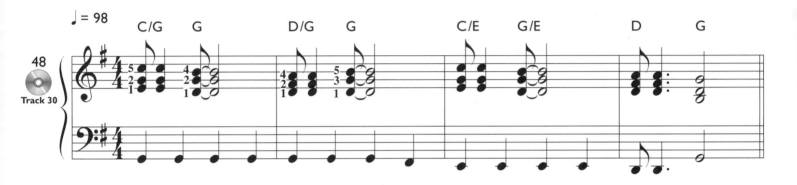

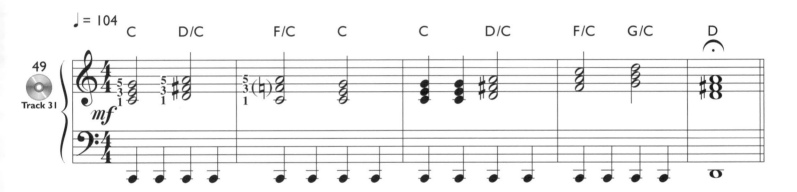

Example 50 uses three different pedal tones.

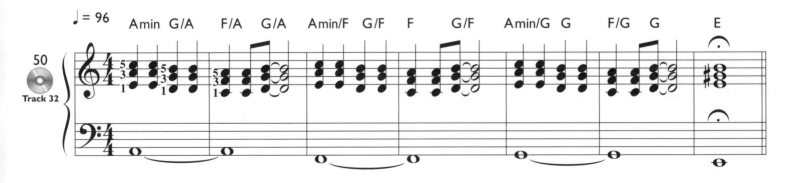

Here is a tune featuring pedal tones. Notice how the pedal tones are indicated in the slash chords; in the first four measures, there is always a "C" to the right of the slash.

BLUE FIRE

Track 33

D.C. stands for *da capo*, which is Italian meaning "return to the top." *Al coda* means jump to the *Coda* (ending section) when you get to the "To Coda" sign ⊕ (second time through).

CHAPTER 7

Reading a Lead Sheet

THREE TYPES OF LEAD SHEETS

Sometimes rock music is written in a sort of rough sketch called a *lead sheet* (also called a *chart*). There are several kinds of lead sheets, and the type we use depends on the situation. Sometimes the melody is shown on a treble clef staff with lyrics below and chords above. Other times, the melody is ignored and just chords are written over slashes that show the number of beats per bar. Another kind of lead sheet shows the chords to play and *rhythmic notation* (a style of music notation that shows only the rhythm and not any specific pitch).

Below is an example of a lead sheet similar to what you might see in a collection of standard tunes. This is the melody-and-chord-only style lead sheet. If this were a true song, lyrics would be shown below the notes.

Here is the same music with slashes instead of the melody. The slashes designate the time in each bar and the player is free to make up a part using the chords above the staff.

The following lead sheet uses rhythmic notation. The player uses the rhythm shown as a guide to where accents should be placed. The diamond shapes and small slashes replace the standard note heads and their placement does not indicate any particular pitch. Stems, and sometimes flags and beams, give the rest of the rhythmic information.

RHYTHMIC NOTATION BASIC NOTE VALUES

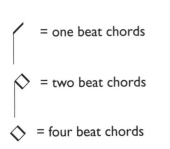

= one beat chords

= two beat chords

= four beat chords

Here is a simple realization of the lead sheet in example 51 using just triads in the left hand.

This simple realization of our four-bar lead sheet would do in a pinch, but the left-hand part is somewhat stiff and muddy sounding. Since lead sheets almost never give the left-hand part, we are challenged to come up with a left-hand part that sounds good and moves the tune forward.

Here is a better suggestion for the left hand with the right hand playing the melody. The circled notes in the right hand are chord tones. This is a good example of how one hand can perform two functions at once: melody and accompaniment. Notice that the left-hand part is kept very simple. It provides a bass of roots and 5ths.

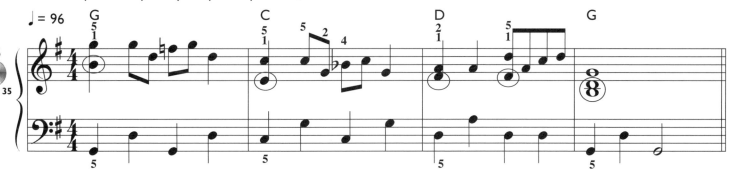

Lead sheets may not be the best way to write music but they are short and simple to read. They provide a good "roadmap" of where a song is going and allow you the freedom to create your own part. Because of its simplicity, a lead sheet can be an aide for memorizing songs, too.

SONG FORM TERMINOLOGY

To understand song *forms* (the form is the organization of the song) and lead sheets, musicians use terms to describe different sections of a song.

The most common terms are: ***intro, verse, chorus*** and ***bridge.***

The ***intro*** is the introduction or beginning of a song.
The ***verse*** is the part of the song that tells the story. Most songs have several verses.
The ***chorus*** is the part of the song that is repeated often and without variation. It summarizes or comments on the point of the story told in the verses.
The ***bridge*** is connecting musical material that is different from the verse and chorus. It adds a contrast to the verse and chorus.

USING LETTERS TO DESCRIBE SONG FORM

Here are two examples of how a song form can be described with letters.

Verse	Verse	Chorus	Verse	Chorus		Verse	Chorus	Verse	Chorus	Bridge	Chorus
A	A	B	A	B	or	A	B	A	B	C	B

Other terms you may see are ***outro*** or ***tag*** or ***Coda***. These are just three different ways to say the same thing: the end of the song. Sometimes a song will have a ***refrain,*** which is like a chorus but shorter, that is often tacked onto the end of the verses. A good example of a refrain is the "Fa-la la-la-la, la-la-la-la" at the end of each verse of *Deck the Halls*.

Here is an example of a more elaborate lead sheet.

RIDING ON THE WIND: MELODY LEAD SHEET

Track 36

The lead sheet for *Riding on the Wind* shows why it is so important to understand how this style of notation works.

FORM FOR *RIDING ON THE WIND*

First, there is a two bar drum solo at the beginning. **DON'T PLAY DURING THE DRUM SOLO.** Drummers get upset if you steal their thunder, and they have hard objects in their hands.

The keyboard comes in at bar 3 and plays only chords up through bar 6.

The verse begins at bar 7. The singer, or lead instrument, would start there. The verse is played twice.

Then the band goes to the B section at measure 15, where the chorus begins.

After the chorus, there is one more verse and then another chorus.

After the last chorus, skip to the Coda and end the song.

Don't overlook the change of key signature from A Minor in the verse to A Major in the chorus.

* The long line in the middle of the staff ├──┤ indicates more than one measure of rest. The number above the staff indicates how many measures of rest.

D.S. = Go back to the sign 𝄋.
al Coda = to the Coda ⊕.

This song uses rhythmic notation. Often, when rehearsing with a band, you won't get as much information as given in the chart shown on page 44. Notice that ties and dots occur in rhythmic notation just as in standard notation.

When playing this chart for the first time, use simple triads in the right hand and single root notes in the left hand. As you become more familiar with the tune, add variations, such as inversions, to the right-hand part.

RIDING ON THE WIND: RHYTHMIC NOTATION LEAD SHEET

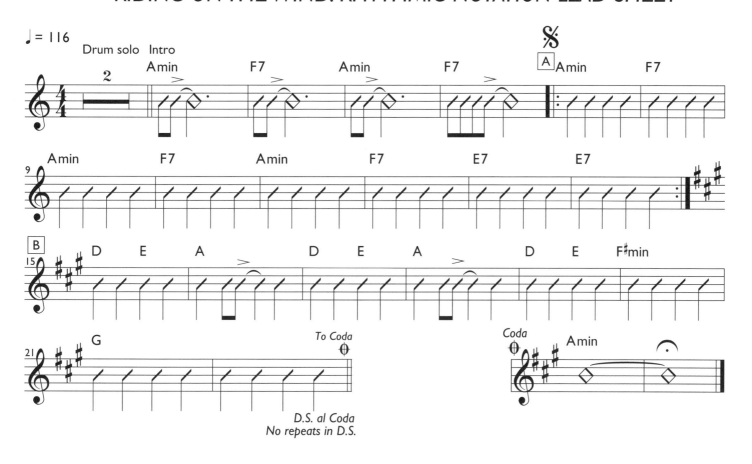

Here is *House of the Rising Sun* as you might see it in a recording session. This chart uses just chords and slashes.

HOUSE OF THE RISING SUN: CHORD AND SLASH LEAD SHEET

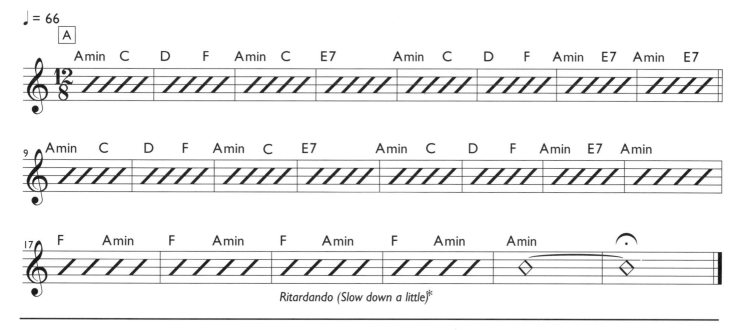

Ritardando (Slow down a little)*

---

* A ritardando is abbreviated rit.

CHAPTER 8

More Left-Hand Patterns

As you know, lead sheets deliberately leave out a left-hand part. Since we know that good rockin' piano needs a strong bass line, here are a few pages of left-hand patterns. They will come in handy when playing from lead sheets.

BOOGIE-WOOGIE PATTERNS

Boogie piano developed in the black urban centers as an outgrowth of the raucous barrelhouse piano of the early 20th century. This style relies on a strong percussive bass line to drive the songs forward and makes you want to move your feet.

Here is another classic left-hand line in quarter notes with the added 7th tone.

Here is a classic left-hand part. Guitar players are particularly fond of this idea, especially in the keys of A or E. On the keyboard, it's easiest in C.

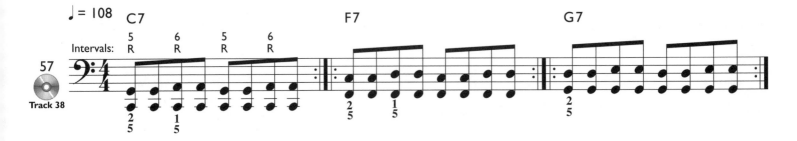

Stevie Wonder was a Motown child prodigy who hit the top of the charts with Fingertips (Pt. 2) *in 1963. He later matured into one of the most influential artists of the 20th century, recording most of the instruments on his dazzling solo albums.*

Here is a boogie pattern in G. Strive to keep the pattern very steady with a solid feel. This pattern uses an A♯, which is the same as (enharmonically equivalent to) B♭. The B♭ is the ♭3, or minor 3rd, in G. This pattern highlights the sound of the minor 3rd moving to the major 3rd (B). This minor/major ambiguity is a big part of the language of blues- and boogie-influenced rock'n'roll.

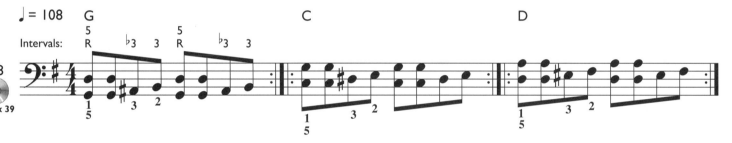

Here is a walking boogie bass line. Let's add a few chord hits to this next pattern. As you add the right hand, keep the left hand very steady.

WALKIN' & TALKIN'

Track 40

The pattern used in *This Rock'n'Roll Thing* will rock the house when played with spirit. Repeat the introduction until *you hit a groove* (where the rhythm starts to feel great!) and then add the right hand part. Pay attention to the first and second endings(see page 11).

THIS ROCK'N'ROLL THING

Track 41

% = Repeat previous measure.

An octave is the interval created between the two closest notes with the same letter name. It gets its name from the root "*oct*" which means "eight." The eighth note of a major scale is an octave above the root. An octave also equals twelve half steps. In keyboard music, octaves are often used to strengthen bass lines in the left hand. They are also used to add emphasis to a melody line in the right hand.

Octaves require extra effort and a little stretching of the fingers, especially for players with small hands. If your hands get tired, stop and rest. Some players have to "roll" their octaves—that is, play the lower note and then immediately jump to the higher note. Try playing a scale in octaves using one hand at a time.

Same fingering throughout.

Same fingering throughout.

At first, it seems logical that all octaves would be played with a 5-1 fingering in the left hand and a 1-5 fingering in the right hand. However, if your hands can stretch far enough, it is sometimes good to use a 4-1 fingering in the left hand and a 1-4 fingering in the right hand when playing on the black keys. This makes it easier to connect notes with lots of octaves in succession. If this feels too difficult, move on and come back to it later.

Here is an A Major scale with 1-4 fingerings on the black keys:

Try a D Major scale in the left hand.

Here are two tunes that feature octaves in the bass.

mp = Mezzo piano. moderately soft.

MILES FROM NOWHERE

Track 42

= Repeat previous two measures.

Almost There features the use of a *sus4 chord* in the 5th measure. In a sus4 chord, the middle note, or 3rd, is raised a half step to the 4th tone above the root. The 4th is called a "suspension" because in 14th century music, you could only get this sound by holding the note over, or suspending it, from a previous chord. In this case, the F♯ (3rd) of the D chord is raised to the G (4th) and suspended as an anticipation of the D chord in bar 6 where the 4th resolves down to the 3rd.

ALMOST THERE

Track 43

= Crescendo.
Play gradually louder.

BROKEN OCTAVES

Octaves can be used to make good, simple bass lines by alternating the pinky and thumb to create a rocking-back-and-forth motion in the left hand. Paul

McCartney of The Beatles used this technique in songs such as *Lady Madonna* and *Martha, My Dear.*

Here are some rocking, broken-octave lines:

ALL NIGHT STATION

Play right hand second time only.

Track 44

Here is a classic boogie-woogie line with octaves.

Billy Powell *is one of the founding members of the Southern rock group, Lynyrd Skynyrd, which was established in the 1970s. His funky, rollicking piano style is an excellent compliment to their bluesy/country guitar leads.*

PHOTO • MARK HARLAN/STARFILES, INC.

If it feels comfortable, you can try playing every other octave with a 4-1 fingering. If you have an acoustic piano or full-size electric keyboard, play the left hand one octave lower than written. Also, notice the key signature: four sharps! E Major is a big rock key. So, take it slow at first but get used to it! Rock on!

SALOON SPIDER
Track 45

CHAPTER 9

Pentatonic Scales and Beginning Improvisation

Rock keyboard players are often part of the *rhythm section*—the group of instruments that accompany the singer or lead instrument. That is why we've concentrated on chords, left-hand bass lines and rhythms. But you may be called upon to take the lead melody or even *improvise* a solo! Improvising is the act of spontaneous invention. In music, that means creating music from your own imagination. If that sounds intimidating, don't panic. There are tools of the trade which make it simple. We'll start with the *pentatonic scales*.

PENTATONIC SCALES

When improvising, musicians often think about scales. We need to know which to use for soloing over the chords being played. Pentatonic scales are used in many rock tunes because they are simple and they fit like a glove over most basic chords.

Pentatonic scales are made up of five notes (*"penta"* is the Greek word for "five"). If you play just the black keys on the piano, you will have a pentatonic scale! (Notice that there are five black keys in every octave). Let's compare the now-familiar major scale with a *major pentatonic* scale.

Here are the C Major and C Major Pentatonic scales:

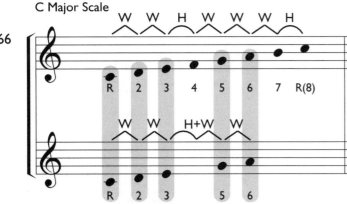

The most tense notes in the major scale are the 4th (in the key of C, that's F) and the 7th (B). Play these notes against a C chord to hear why we think of them as tense. They are both dissonant (they clash) against the chord. The major pentatonic scale eliminates these notes. This is why the C Major Pentatonic scale fits so well with the C Major chord.

The first time through *Deeper River*, play the C Major Pentatonic tune written out for the right hand. In the repeat, continue to play notes from the pentatonic scale randomly. The more you play, the easier it will become. Sometimes it helps to let two bars of left-hand accompaniment go by before beginning to improvise. This will help you solidify the left-hand part and get a feel for the rhythm.

Try combining longer notes (quarter notes and half notes) with shorter notes (eighth notes) to create interesting rhythms for your improvisation.

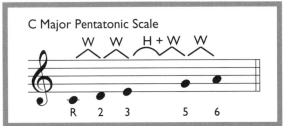

C Major Pentatonic Scale

 **DEEPER RIVER**

Track 46

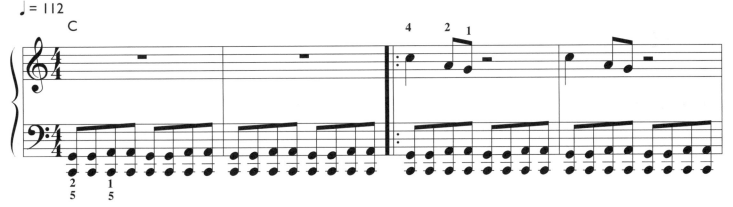

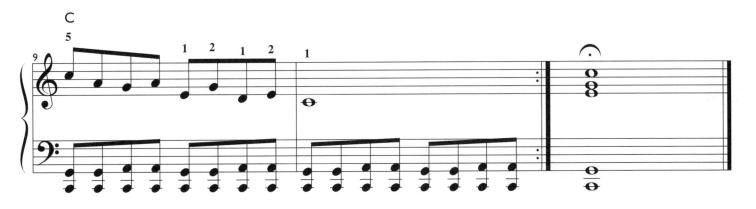

In Example 67, the right hand plays three C Major Pentatonic *phrases*. A phrase is a complete musical thought. The music is like a little conversation, and the phrases are the sentences. Play the three written phrases and then improvise a fourth. Create a melody similar to the other three using the C Major Pentatonic scale. You get the last word in the conversation! Don't worry: you can play any note in the scale. There are no "wrong notes" as long as you stay in the scale. Experiment with different rhythms, and don't be afraid to leave a little space (rests) in your melody. If you have trouble being spontaneous, try writing a melody on the staff.

Let's do it again, but this time in G and with two long phrases instead of four short phrases.

In this example, we use a different pentatonic scale for each chord. When the left hand plays a G chord, we play notes from the G Major Pentatonic scale. Over the C chord, we play the C Major Pentatonic. The chords to a song are often called *the changes*. Changing scales as the chords change is called *playing the changes*.

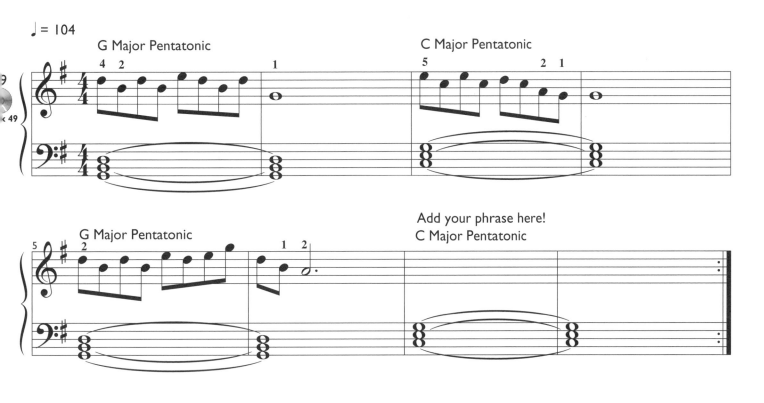

Chuck Leavell is a excellent keyboardist who made his reputation with the Allman Brothers Band. Since the 1970s, he has played with Eric Clapton, the Black Crowes and the Rolling Stones.

Let's play the changes some more, but in the key of F with two new pentatonic scales: F and B♭. You're on your own—no tune has been provided. Improvise with gusto!

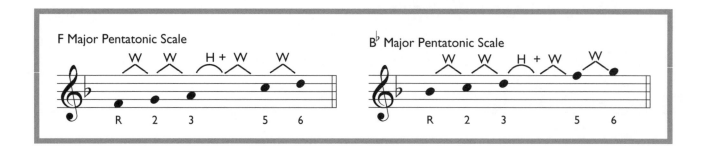

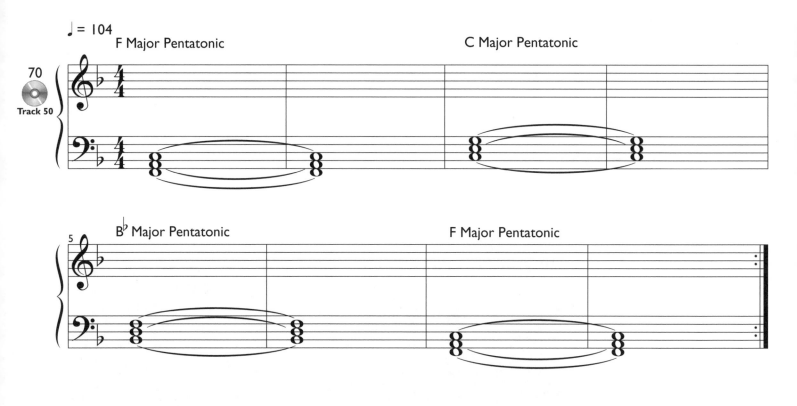

You can also play the major pentatonic scale of the key of the song all the way through, as we did on pages 55 and 56. After you play Example 71 with the suggested scale on each chord, try playing just the F Major Pentatonic scale throughout. Listen to how well the notes fit, even as the chords change. This is called *diatonic* improvisation (see page 71 for an explanation of diatonic).

In *Far As You Like*, try to determine where the pentatonic scales are changing with the chords. In the repeat of the A section, improvise your own melody in the right hand using these scales:

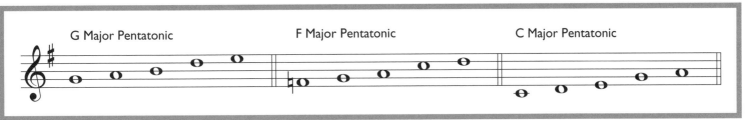

G Major Pentatonic   F Major Pentatonic   C Major Pentatonic

FAR AS YOU LIKE

Track 51

The minor pentatonic and major pentatonic scales are closely related but they sound very different. The major pentatonic scale has a country-music flavor but the minor pentatonic scale has a darker, bluesier sound. They are similar in that they both have five notes but they compare differently to the major scale.

Here is a C Major scale and a C Minor Pentatonic scale. Notice that the 3rd and 7th of the minor pentatonic scale are flatted (♭3 and ♭7).

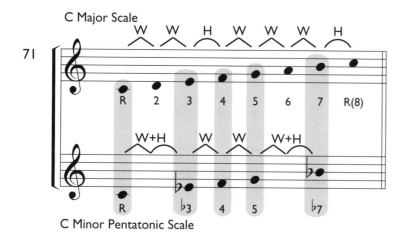

C Major Scale

71

C Minor Pentatonic Scale

Here is a comparison of the C Major Pentatonic and the A Minor Pentatonic scales. The minor pentatonic scale is related to the major pentatonic scale in the same way that the natural minor scale is related to the major scale (see page 18).

The root of the A Minor Pentatonic scale is built on 6 of the major pentatonic scale. It is a minor 3rd below the root of the C Major Pentatonic. A Minor Pentatonic and C Major Pentatonic have the exact same notes. Played in a different order, though, they sound completely different. Cool!

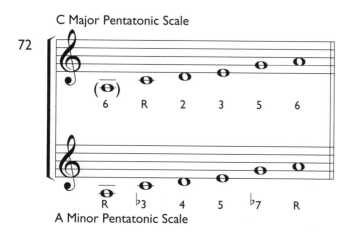

C Major Pentatonic Scale

72

A Minor Pentatonic Scale

To get a feeling for the minor pentatonic scale, learn to play *New Life*. Notice the key signature. This tune is in the key of C Minor.

NEW LIFE

Track 52

Billy Joel became a recording artist for Columbia Records in the 1970s. He is one of the most popular pianists in the world. His tour with superstar/pianist Elton John was a piano aficionados dream.

PHOTO • LYDIA CRISS/COURTESY OF STARFILES, INC.

Off the Main Highway uses the E Minor Pentatonic scale for the main melody. Notice that, except for the first two measures and the last, the song is repeated three times. Improvise your own melody over the repeats using the E Minor Pentatonic scale. Remember, you do not have to stay in the same octave as you improvise. Feel free to move the E Minor Pentatonic scale to different octaves. Have fun!

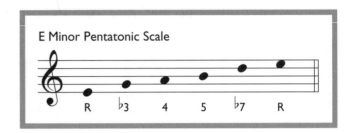

 OFF THE MAIN HIGHWAY

Track 53

CHAPTER 10

The Blues

Blues music is at the heart of lots of great rock'n'roll. In fact, one could argue that if there were never blues music, rock'n'roll would never have developed. Rock music grew out of rhythm and blues in the 1950s, so, much of what we hear as rock music is really blues with a different beat.

THE BLUES SCALE AND BLUE NOTES

The major and minor pentatonic scales you learned in the last chapter are great tools for blues improvisation, and so is the *blues scale*. On the right, the C Blues scale is compared with the C Major scale. The C Blues scale is very similar to the C Minor Pentatonic scale except that it includes an additional flat 5 (♭5). The ♭5 is a very distinctive sound. It adds such an important twist to the blues sound that it is often called a *blue note*. Sometimes, for reasons of convenience, the ♭5 is written as a ♯4, its enharmonic equivalent.

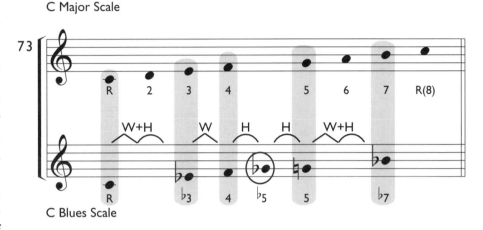

C Major Scale

C Blues Scale

73

Here is a typical blues melody using the ♭5:

♩ = 96

Since blues harmony is more open to experimentation than many other musical styles, the blues performer has much more leeway in choosing notes for a solo. Quite often, the blues will freely combine major and minor sounds (major 3rds and minor 3rds) in a piece of music. The left hand might play harmony based on major chords while the right hand, or the soloist, plays a melody that is based on the minor chord! The minor 3rd (♭3) played against a major chord is another very important blue note.

Here is a short blues passage in G that typifies this combination of major (in the left hand) and minor (in the right hand).

♩ = 92   C

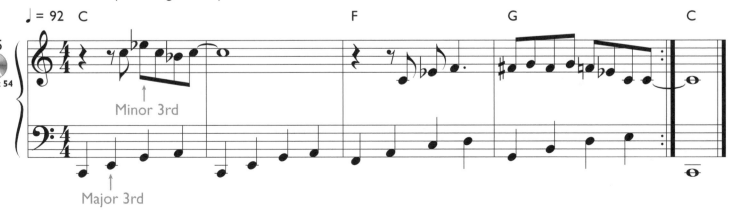

Minor 3rd

Major 3rd

See The Light demonstrates the use of the ♭5 in the key of E Minor.

SEE THE LIGHT

Track 55

Fine

Da Capo al Fine means to return to the beginning and play up until the *Fine*.

D.C. al Fine **
*Hold last time only

THE GRACE NOTE

The *grace note* is like the spice in Louisiana cooking—a tiny bit goes a long way. Grace notes are little notes that precede a larger note called the *main note*. The two notes are usually connected with a small slur marking. To play a grace note, rob a bit of time from the main note and quickly play it before the main note. Some blues players actually slide their finger off the grace note on to the main note, especially if the grace note falls on a black key. Fingerings such as this are marked with a dash; 3-3 indicates to slide the 3rd finger from one key to the next (see example 76).

To prepare for grace notes, play the exercise below. Notice that the ♭5 blue note is sometimes written as A♯ (if it is ascending) and sometimes as B♭ (if it is descending).

76
Track 56

This time, three of the blue notes are shortened to become grace notes. In each case, quickly slide your finger off the black key to the white key. Don't worry about being rhythmically precise with the grace notes. There is some rhythmic freedom allowed in this style. The main thing is to have fun and "get the blues."

77
Track 57

So far, all the eighth notes you have played have been *straight eighths*. That is, all the eighths were played evenly. The beats were evenly divided in two. There is another style of eighth notes called *swing eighths*. Swing eighths divide the beats into uneven eighth notes—the first eighth is held for about double the value of the second. We would say that music played with swing eighths is in *swing feel* or *shuffle feel*. Jazz musicians almost always play in swing feel, imitating the era of the great big band swing era. Early rock performers borrowed this feel, usually calling it a shuffle. It is an infectious beat and easy to feel, but there are special conventions for reading and writing them that you must learn.

Let's start by looking at a measure of straight eighths and a measure of eighth-note triplets.

The next example shows swing eighths. In the first measure, the first two notes of each triplet are tied together. Count aloud "1-&-ah, 2-&-ah," etc. Clap on the numbers and the "ah's." In the second measure, the eighth notes look like straight eighths, but are counted and performed as swing eighths. Count and clap again. It should sound exactly like the first measure. That's right! Swing eighths look just like straight eighths. The important difference is the "Swing 8ths" mark above the music.

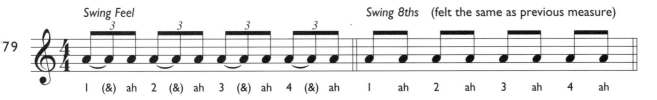

Sometimes the marking above the music will say "Swing Feel," or "Shuffle." In jazz music, those terms are often left out because the player assumes the music is in typical jazz swing feel. The reason for this predicament is that writing all the music in triplets would clutter up the page with little "3s." It's just tidier to do it this way.

Here are two ways of playing a typical left-hand part, first with straight eighths and then with swing eighths:

Let's play an old time rockin' shuffle in D. Practice each hand separately. Play very slowly at first to make sure both hands are coordinated. Keep a steady, driving beat throughout.

ROADHOUSE DELUXE

Track 60

♩ = 104

Swing 8ths

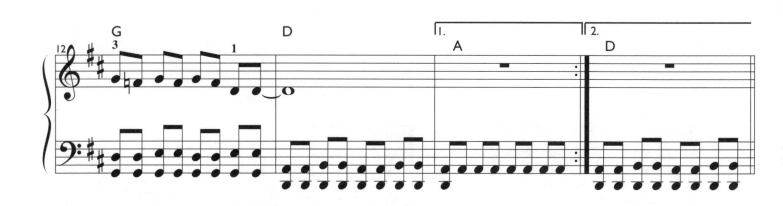

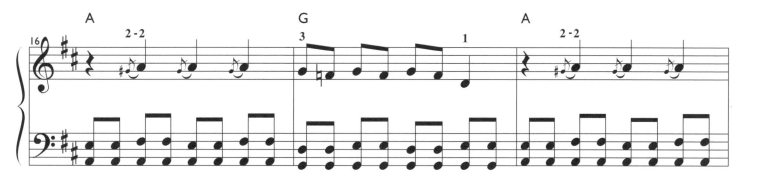

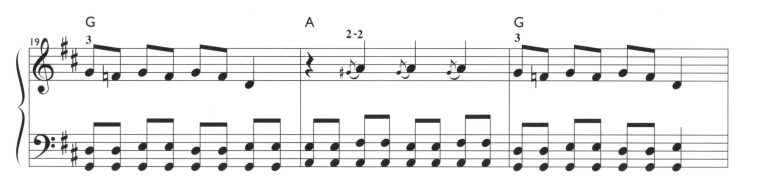

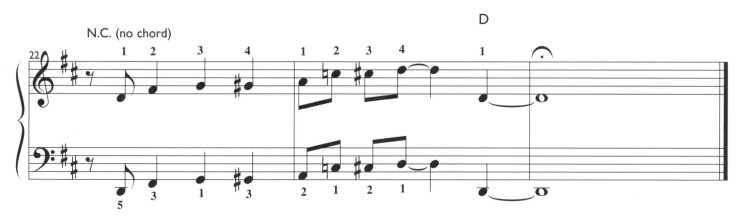

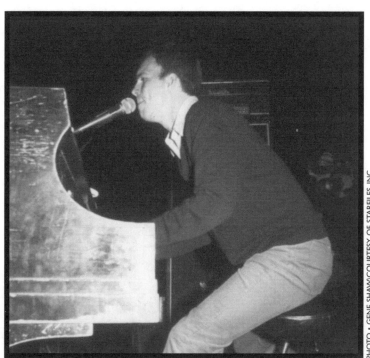

Ben Folds of the Ben Folds Five is one of the hottest young pianists in contemporary music. With their hit CD, "Whatever and Ever Amen," released in 1997, they became well known throughout the music world. Ben Folds is an accomplished player capable of everything from tender ballads to hard rocking psuedo-punk.

Here is a tune with a boogie bass line in the left hand. Concentrate on keeping the left hand steady as you play the melody in the right hand. If you play this with the proper attitude (rockin'!), your hands may get tired. If so, rest your hands a bit and play again with even *more* spirit! Seriously, you should be careful to avoid an overuse injury.

HONKY TONK TOWN

Track 61

Here is a honky-tonk shuffle. Feel free to embellish the right hand with grace notes. That's right! Put 'em in wherever the spirit moves you.

NO EASY RIDERS

Track 62

*Last time only.

DIATONIC TRIADS

In order to understand how the blues really works, we must learn about *diatonic triads*. Diatonic means "of the scale," so diatonic triads are those triads that come from the scale. Each scale degree has its own chord which is assigned a Roman numeral. Notice that in "Diatonic Triads in C" below, each note of the scale becomes the root of a chord.

Here is a quick review of upper case and lower case Roman numerals showing their Arabic equivalents.

Roman Numerals							
Upper case:	I	II	III	IV	V	VI	VII
Lower case:	I	ii	iii	iv	v	vi	vii
Arabic:	1	2	3	4	5	6	7

Upper case Roman numerals are used to indicate major chords. Lower case Roman numerals are used to indicate minor or diminished* chords.

DIATONIC TRIADS IN C

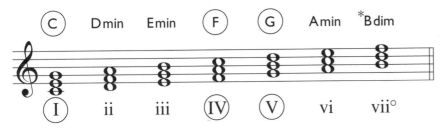

The first (I), fourth (IV) and fifth (V) chords of the major scale are the most important chords in blues and rock music. Literally thousands of songs contain only these three *primary chords*. As long as we've got the primary chords, rock'n'roll will never die!

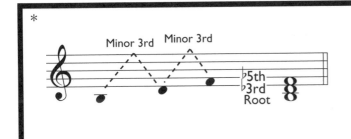

Notice the vii° sign under the last chord in Example 83. The little circle means "diminished." A diminished triad, written *dim*, is made up of two minor 3rds stacked above the root. The diminished triad occurs naturally on the 7th degree of the major scale. Play the diminished triad shown. It has a very distinctive flavor.

The concept of diatonic chords can be carried into all key signatures. Here are the diatonic triads for the D Major scale.

DIATONIC TRIADS IN D

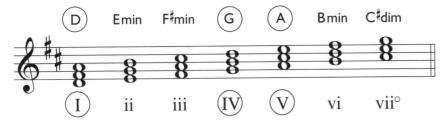

Practice the diatonic chords in all key signatures, building a triad on each note of the scale. You'll find all the major scales on page 95 of this book, and a helpful chart of the primary chords in every key on page 72.

THE TWELVE-BAR BLUES

Most blues songs, and most blues-based rock songs, have a structure we call the *twelve-bar blues*. Obviously, the form is twelve bars long! The form can be repeated as many times as you like. Each time through the twelve-bar form is called a *chorus*.

Using Roman numerals to identify the chords, here is the formula for a basic twelve-bar blues:

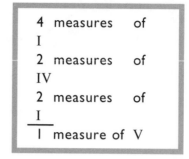

4 measures of I
2 measures of IV
2 measures of I
1 measure of V

This chord pattern is the universal language of the blues, and all rock players should know it in all key signatures. Here is a twelve-bar blues in G:

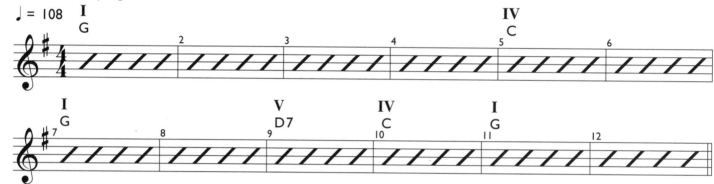

For practice, play this blues with simple triads.

TRANSPOSING

Using the Roman numerals, it is possible to move this chord progression to any key. This is called *transposing*. You can start on any triad and apply this formula, and you'll be playing the blues. Every day, try playing this pattern in another key. Follow the cycle of 5ths (see page 15) order. A seasoned player will know the blues in any key.

The following chart will help you play the blues in any key:

PRIMARY CHORDS IN ALL TWELVE KEYS

Major Key	I	IV	V
C	C	F	G
G	G	C	D
D	D	G	A
A	A	D	E
E	E	A	B
B	B	E	F♯
G♭	G♭	C♭	D♭
D♭	D♭	G♭	A♭
A♭	A♭	D♭	E♭
E♭	E♭	A♭	B♭
B♭	B♭	E♭	F
F	F	B♭	C

VARIATIONS ON THE TWELVE-BAR BLUES

Often, players will spruce up the standard twelve-bar blues (example 83) with variations. The form is still twelve measures long, but other chords will be substituted for the basic chords.

THE QUICK FOUR

This first pattern moves to the IV chord in the second measure. This common blues variation is sometimes called a "quick four." The rest of the chords remain the same. Notice that to get a true blues sound, we use dominant 7th chords throughout.

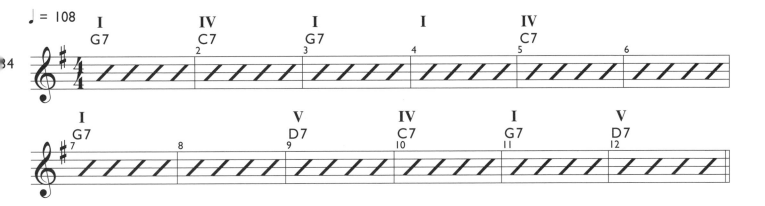

THE DIM7 CONNECTOR

The following blues uses a diminished 7 chord (dim7). It is similar to the diminished chord we looked at on page 71, except another minor 3rd is added on top. The added note is a $\flat$7 above the root. The formula for the chord is root, $\flat$3, $\flat$5, $\flat$7.

In this variation, simply raising the root of the IV chord by one half step creates the dim7 chord; the IV chord (C7) becomes $\sharp$iv° (C$\sharp$dim7). The C$\sharp$dim7 is spelled C$\sharp$ (root), E ($\flat$3), G ($\flat$5) and B$\flat$ ($\flat$7). The diminished 7 chord often makes for an all-purpose transition chord. That is, it will act as a connector chord from one simple chord to another. In this case, it is a great connector from IV back to I.

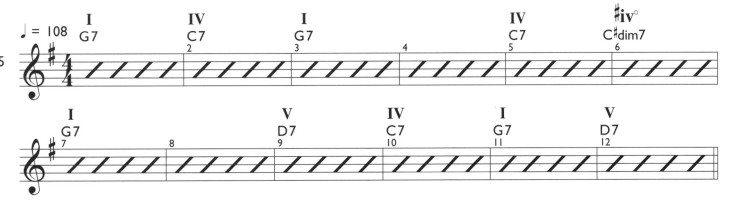

THE CYCLE OF 5THS

Very often, musicians will use the cycle of 5ths (see page 15) to create interesting chord progressions. In the blues, you can approach I, IV or V with chords from outside the key that relate via the cycle of 5ths. For instance, in G, you can approach the V chord (D7) like this: E7, A7, D7. The A7 is not in the key, but it is a 5th above the D7. The E7, which is not in the key either, is a 5th above the A7. Even though E7 and A7 are not in the key, they work because of the cycle of 5ths. Notice that when V (D7) moves to I (G7) the cycle of 5ths is continued.

E7
5th ↘ A7
5th ↓
5th ↙ D7
G7

This song uses straight blues changes with a moving bass line in the first chorus. In this chorus, you are accompanying (*comping*). Notice the slash chords that appear at the ends of the measures. These quick *passing chords* add a nice twist. In the second chorus you solo. Between bars 22 and 24, a cycle of 5ths is used to approach the V chord. Enjoy the sound!

TAKE TO THE ROAD

Track 63

1st Chorus Comping

When blues riffs are used in the left hand, they can be the basis of some very hot bass lines. Play a C7 chord in the right hand and try the left-hand line in example 86.

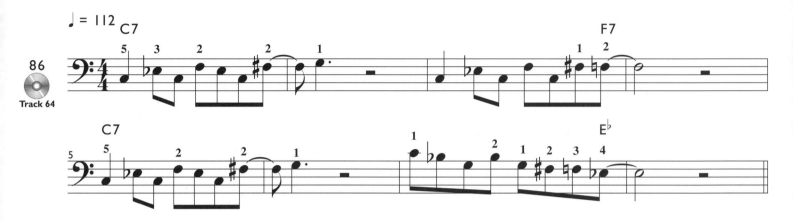

To get even more power out of a blues riff, double the notes with the right hand one octave higher. Notice that both hands are playing in bass clef.

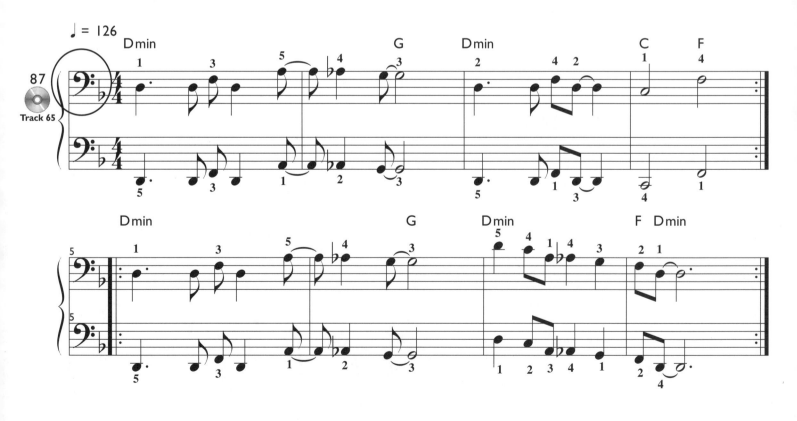

Try doubling this bass line with your right hand.

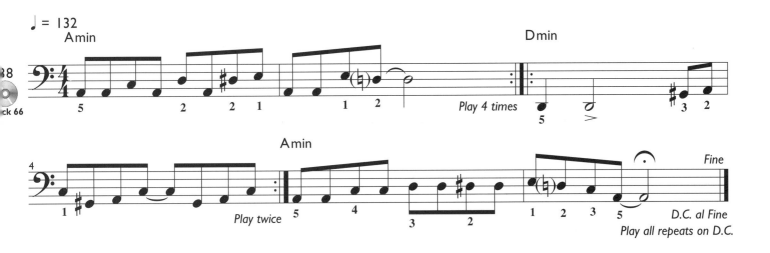

In the A section, double the bass line with your right hand. In the B section, play the triads indicated above the staff. In bars 8 and 12, go back to doubling the bass line with your right hand.

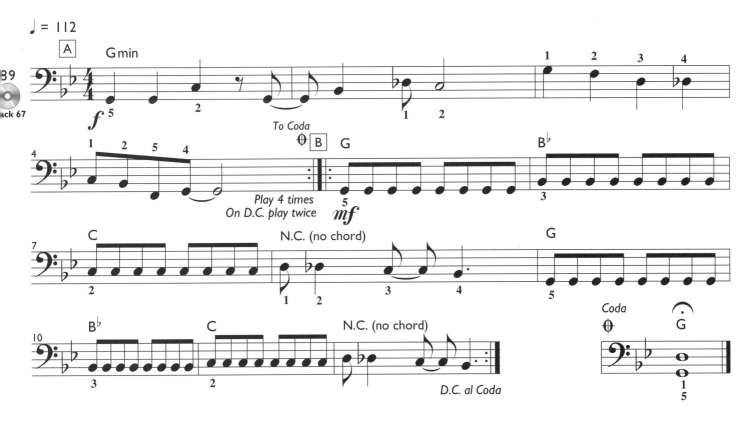

CHAPTER 11

Funky Sixteenths

Most early rock was based around straight- or swing-eighth notes. They are usually easy to play, read and understand. This chapter deals with sixteenth-note rhythms.

In the late 1960s and into the 1970s, pop music became more rhythmically complex. Sixteenth-note rhythms became more common. Listeners and dancers, in particular, really liked what sixteenths did to the beat. It added "the FUNK." The soul music explosion of the late 1960s (Motown) moved this style to the forefront of rock and pop music. Rock players were looking for new ways of making *the groove* happen.

Here is a typical bass part using only eighth notes:

♩ = 104

90

Track 68

It is a perfectly good bass line. It has a strong root feel and moves things along. But suppose it's the last set of the night, the bass player gets a little punchy and holds the first note of the line just one quarter beat too long. This is what happens:

♩ = 104

91

Track 69

All of a sudden the bass line starts getting a little loose! The drummer senses what's going on and starts hitting a fat back beat (strong accents on the 2nd and 4th beats). People start dancing like crazy and a new style of music is born!

Sixteenth notes look more formidable than they are. All you have to do is divide the beat into four parts instead of two. They are twice as fast as eighth notes. The next example compares eighth notes and sixteenths. For the sixteenth notes, count "1-e-&-ah, 2-e-&-ah, 3-e-&-ah, 4-e-&-ah."

♩ = 80   8th Notes (Two per beat)   16th Notes (Four per beat)

92

At first, play sixteenth-note passages slowly to insure accuracy. Check Chapter 13 in this book for some sixteenth-note ballads—ballads are slow!

To play repeating sixteenths at a faster tempo, some special techniques can be utilized. The next example shows a way of alternating fingers, right and left, to play rapidly. This method is especially great if you need a rapid, machine-gun-style riff.

♩ = 96

93

Such rapid passages are unusual in rock songs. They are sometimes novelty parts, or a bit of flash to see how quickly the keyboardist can play. More practical are syncopated parts where the keyboardist breaks up the pattern with off-beat accents to make a tune really groove.

Below is a bass line written in two different ways. First, it is written over two measures in eighth notes, then in one measure with sixteenth notes. The two versions will sound identical but in the second version, the beats move twice as slow. This is called *half time*. It takes up half the space and is the way funk lines are usually written.

> = Accent. Play this note louder.

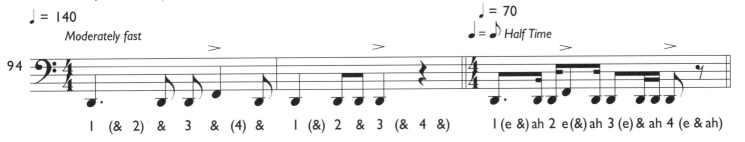

Here is a variation on the bass line from example 94 with variations in the right hand part. Notice the intensive use of syncopation. Syncopation with sixteenths is what funk rhythms are all about.

EXPLOSIVE SOUL

Track 70

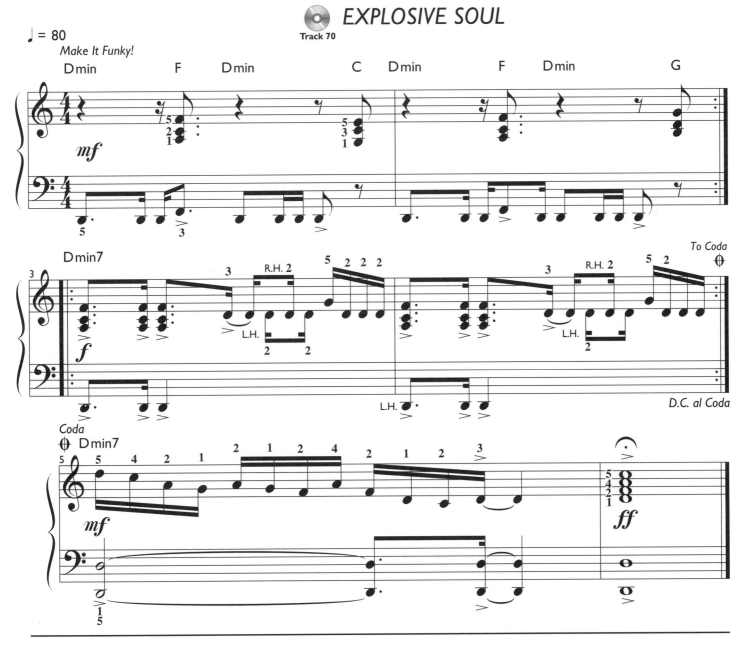

CHAPTER 12

In A Modal Mood

The ancient Greeks believed the different modes affected human psychology in particular ways and used them in many ceremonies and celebrations. The Roman Catholic church codified them in the 9th century. Now, they are considered hip scales for rock and jazz improvisation. Nobody in ancient Greece would have laid odds on *that* ever happening!

A mode is a reordering of a scale which is then thought of as the *parent scale*. If we play a parent scale starting and ending on something other than the 1st degree, we are playing a mode of the scale. Modes force us to approach harmony in new ways and quite often, the music takes on an unusual quality.

Let's take a look at the C Major scale, also called the Ionian mode, and how six other modes are derived from it through reordering.

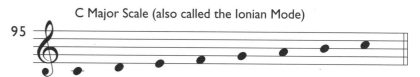
C Major Scale (also called the Ionian Mode)

MODES OF THE MAJOR SCALE

The **Dorian** mode is built on the 2nd step of the major scale.

Dorian Mode

The **Phrygian** mode starts on the 3rd step of a major scale.

Phrygian Mode

The **Lydian** mode is built on the 4th step of the major scale.

Lydian Mode

The **Mixolydian** mode is built on the 5th step of the major scale.

Mixolydian Mode

The **Aeolian** mode is built on the 6th step of the major scale (identical to the natural minor scale).

Aeolian Mode

The **Locrian** mode is built on the 7th step of the major scale.

Locrian Mode

Modes are more often used in contemporary jazz. They are an important method for getting away from more commonly used scales. They add a fresh attitude to the music. We will look into the Dorian and Mixolydian modes since they are the most widely used in rock music.

THE DORIAN MODE

The great jam-tunes of Santana are among the most famous examples of the Dorian mode in rock music. Below is a Dorian tribute to that group. Lowering the 3rd and 7th of a major scale (♭3 and ♭7) will create a Dorian mode.

The first time through *Pure Magic*, play the melody. The second time through, use your right hand to improvise using the D Dorian mode. In the fourth and last repetition, play the written melody again.

Note: Modal pieces use the key signature of the parent scale. So, the key signature for D Dorian is C Major (no sharps or flats.

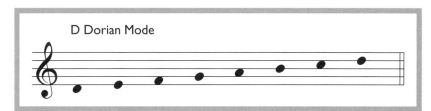

*Hold last time only

Play 4 times

THE MIXOLYDIAN MODE

The Mixolydian mode is just like the major scale except for the seventh tone, which is a minor 7th ($\flat$7) instead of a major 7th (7). Many bands, such as Phish, have done extended jams in the Mixolydian mode.

Here is a tune in C Mixolydian. The C Mixolydian mode fits like a glove around the C7 chord because both include a $\flat$7.

ff = *Fortissimo. Very Loud.*

Finger Substitutions

The 2-1 fingering in the left hand of bar 2 indicates a finger substitution. While holding the key down, move 2 off and replace it with 1.

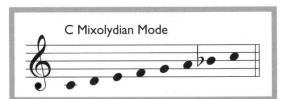

82   Chapter 12—In A Modal Mood

Switch-a-Roo uses two Mixolydian modes: G Mixolydian and E Mixolydian. The G Mixolydian is used with the G7 chords and the E Mixolydian with the E7 chords. Improvise your own solo in the right hand during the second and third times through the A section.

CHAPTER 13

Rock Ballads

There comes a time when even the wildest rockers have to show their sensitive sides. Even hardcore punk rockers like Green Day have come up with sensitive ballads such as *Time of Your Life*, which made their music accessible to a wider audience, reviving their career. Now is the time to put the spotlight on that time-honored tradition: the rock ballad. Yes, it's that time of the night—the slow dance—when you can get romantic with your date.

Let's look back at the styles of the first rock ballads. Following are variations on early rock ballads. The first two recall 1950s doo-wop music.

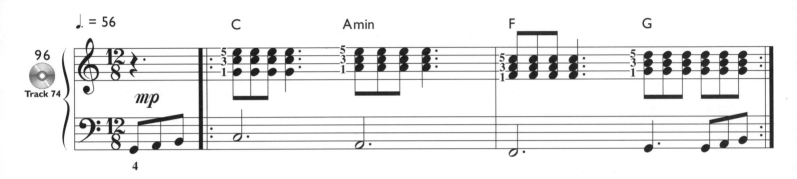

ROLL ON

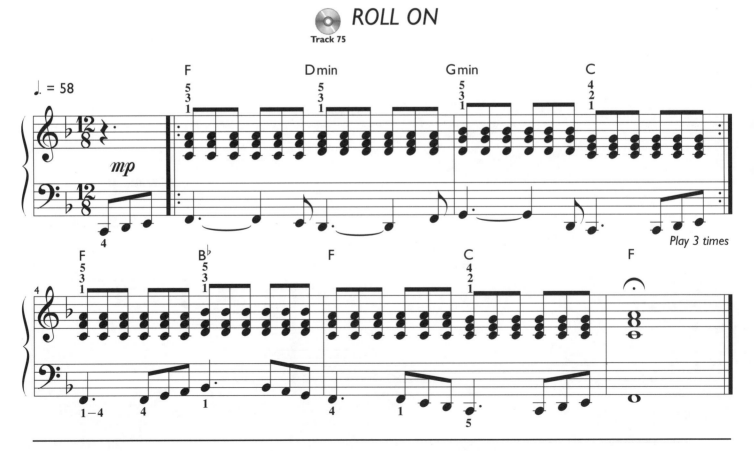

Ballad playing calls upon many different techniques such as block chords (or *pads* as they are often called), arpeggios, fills between the vocal line and others. *Lady Diamond* uses block chords.

pp = Pianissimo. Very Soft.

Track 76

LADY DIAMOND

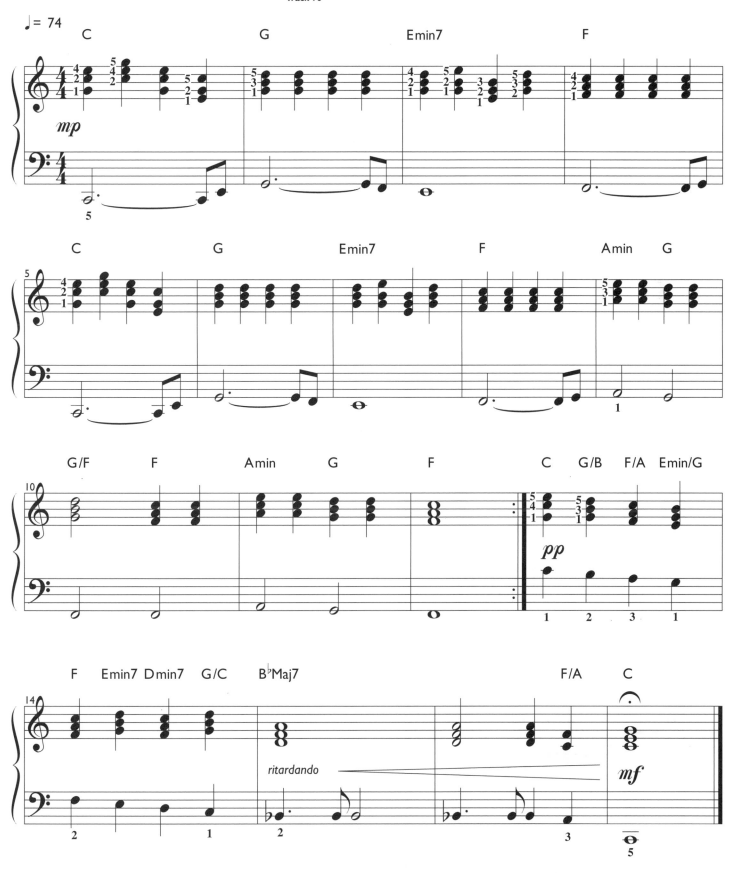

PEDAL TECHNIQUE

We've not used the *sustain pedal* so far in this book. On a standard piano, the right-most pedal is the sustain pedal. Electric keyboards often come with a single pedal for sustain. In most rock and blues music, the rhythms should be as crisp and hard edged as possible. In ballads, we can lush it up a bit.

Try the technique. Play a chord and then depress the pedal. Play a second chord. Release the pedal slightly afterwards, so the chords connect but don't ring together for more than an instant. This keeps the chord change clear and clean. Whatever you do, never just keep the pedal down all the time. It would muddy things considerably.

Damper (or Sustain) Pedal Markings:

Pedal down →

Pedal up

Overlapping Pedal:
As the hand goes down the foot comes up. Pedal again immediately.

This ballad uses sixteenth notes in the right hand. This tune is played very slowly, and the sixteenths should flow smoothly. Notice the use of arpegios in the intro and coda, and pay special attention to the changing time signatures in the intro.

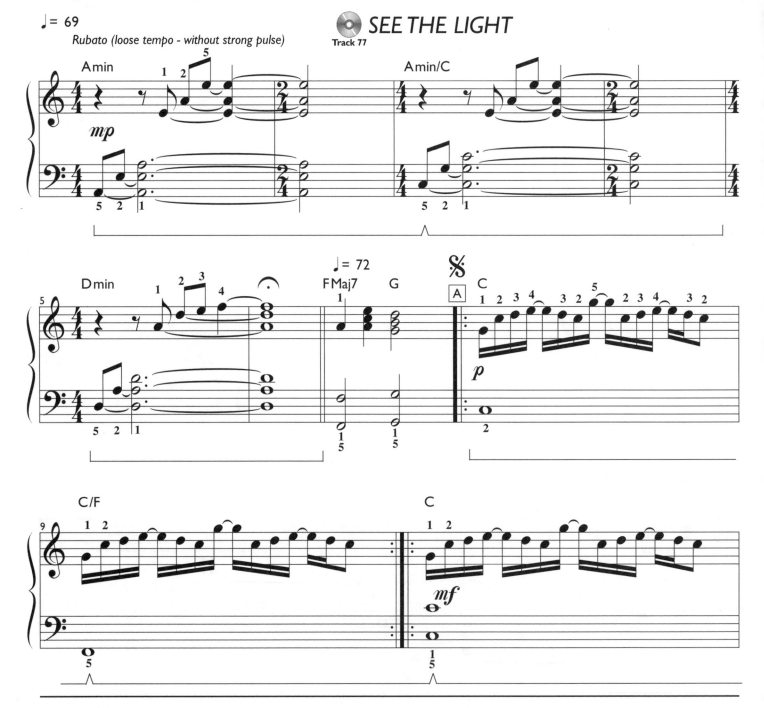

SEE THE LIGHT
Track 77

CHAPTER 14

Electronic Keyboards

ELECTRIC PIANO

Before the advent of pickups for concert grand pianos and the sampled grand piano, the only way a piano could compete with the roar of a rock band at full tilt was with an electric piano.

The first electric pianos were by Wurlitzer. They had a nicely distorted sound. Ray Charles played one in his hit song *Wha'd I Say* to great effect and the Wurlitzer enjoyed great popularity as a result. It wasn't long before Mr. Rhodes invented the Fender-Rhodes piano. The Doors used the Fender-Rhodes on their "LA Woman" album. Since vintage sounds always have an appeal, it is worthwhile to look at the special characteristics of the electric piano.

Generally, electric pianos have fewer keys than a full-size piano. If you have an electric piano sound on your keyboard, try it with the next two tunes. They will sound fine on an acoustic piano but to get the right effect, you should have an electric piano. Notice the accents in the left hand. When played on the old Wurlitzer-type pianos, they would distort nicely and give the tune a great, funky sound.

LUCKY
Track 78

PING PONG

THE ROCK ORGAN: THE MINI AND THE MIGHTY

THE COMBO ORGAN

Similar to the electric piano in size, the combo organ became an integral part of the rock sound in the 1960s. The Doors, Paul Revere and the Raiders, The Dave Clark Five and The Beatles (at Shea Stadium) all used the combo organs by companies such as Farfisa, Gibson and Vox.

The sound of the combo organs varies from brand to brand, so there's room for lots of experimentation as you search for similar sounds on your electronic keyboard. One of the nice things about those keyboards is that the output jack is the same quarter-inch phono jack as on a guitar, so guitar effects pedals can be used to alter the sound. Try a distortion or a chorus pedal for a change of tone.

Here are some typical combo organ licks:

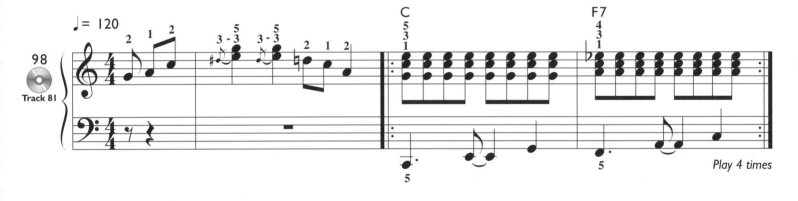

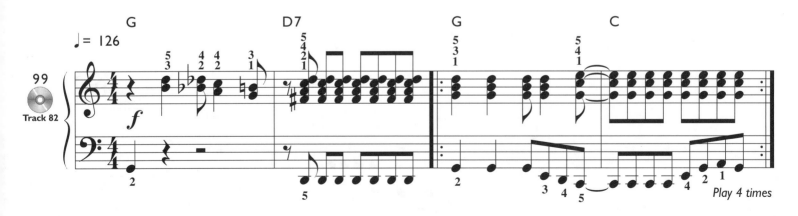

THE MIGHTY HAMMOND ORGAN

The Hammond organs, particularly the B3 and the C3 models, are classic keyboards whose sounds remain very popular today. The richness of their tones, coming from the old analog "tone generators," coupled with spinning Leslie speakers, grease the gears that keep the rock rolling along.

From the first moment the big chords in the intro hit in this typical Hammond-type tune, the listener knows it's party time! It's in the style of The Spencer Davis Group. Have fun!

GOOD TIME COMIN'

Track 83

CHAPTER 15

More Fun Stuff: Keyboard Effects

Every rock instrument makes certain distinctive sounds that have become part of the rock language. The keyboard is no exception. In this chapter, we will look at some of those effects.

SPEED

Some rock keyboard players play ultra-fast sixteenth notes. The ability to play rapidly is partly a matter of natural talent and partly a matter of *technique*. In this sense, "technique" refers to physical advantage through optimum position and use of the hands and fingers.

If you ever have the opportunity to observe any of the rock piano masters close up, such as Jerry Lee Lewis and Little Richard, you will notice that they sometimes angle their hands slightly to the side, favoring the pinky or 5th finger. It almost looks like a karate-chop hand position. This reduces tension, promoting a loose-feeling hand. It also allows for a quicker rebound on the fast notes (see the photo below).

Try applying this hand position to the next example. Play slowly at first and build confidence with the fingerings for the triplets. Then build up to the very brisk suggested tempo. Focus on the hand position!

Holding the hand on an angle can help speed.

The *glissando*, which is sometimes referred to as a *gliss* or *slide*, is a classic keyboard effect. It is a rapid scale passage performed by sliding the hands over the keys. Here are some possible ways to gliss:

1) Use the back of the middle finger (3) to ascend.
2) Use the back of the thumb (1) to descend.
3) Use the palm of the hand in a kind of smear effect going down or up the keys.
4) Use multiple fingers (thumb and middle finger) for a *harmony gliss effect* (more than one note being glissed by one hand simultaneously).

Be careful not to skin the back of your thumb, especially if you get over-excited when rockin' at full tilt. If that becomes a problem for you, use the palm of your hand instead of a single finger. It is less likely to become injured.

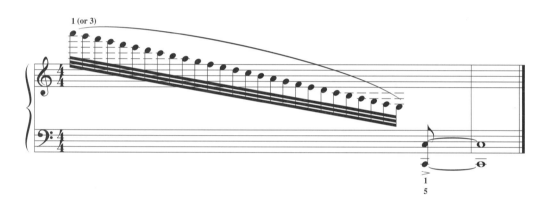

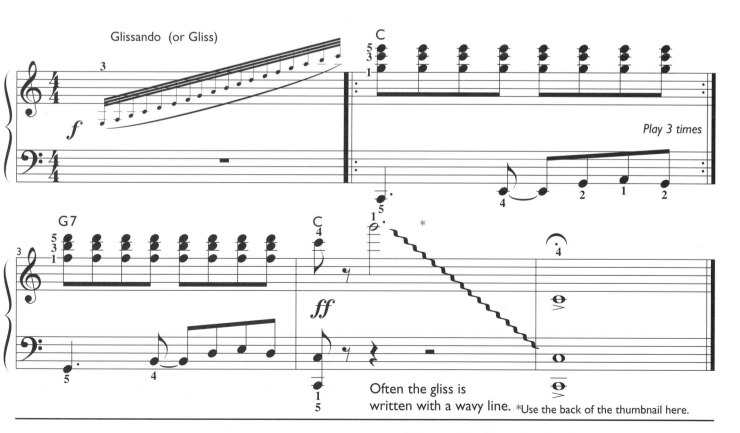

Often the gliss is written with a wavy line. *Use the back of the thumbnail here.

THE TONE CLUSTER: A THUNDEROUS EFFECT!

Using the palm or the side of the hand to play as many notes as possible creates an *atonal* (without a tonal center or key) *tone cluster*. This can also be done using the elbow, or both elbows (!) on the keyboard. Some punk rockers have been known to sit on the keyboard! Hey—whatever works for you is cool. Using tone clusters in your solos gives you an excuse for hitting a **ton** of wrong notes!

Here are some tone clusters to try:

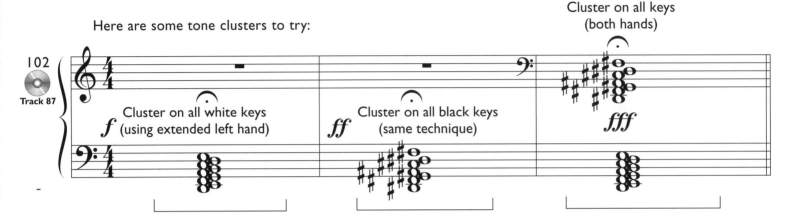

Chords From Yonder uses tone clusters in the right hand. Use your extended right-hand thumb and palm to grab all the notes from A to A for the tone clusters. Pay attention to the dynamic markings.

CHORDS FROM YONDER

Track 88

Playing rock piano is a lifelong project that will give you a sense of accomplishment and lots of enjoyment. This book got you started with the basic tools. By now, you are a rockin' keyboard player. There's a lot left to learn, though, so pick up a copy of *Intermediate Rock Keyboards* and keep the music going. Have fun!

APPENDIX

The Major Scales

Practice these scales as a warm up every time you sit down at the keyboard. Ascending and descending. They are great for keeping your fingers limber and aid the understanding of key signatures and harmony.

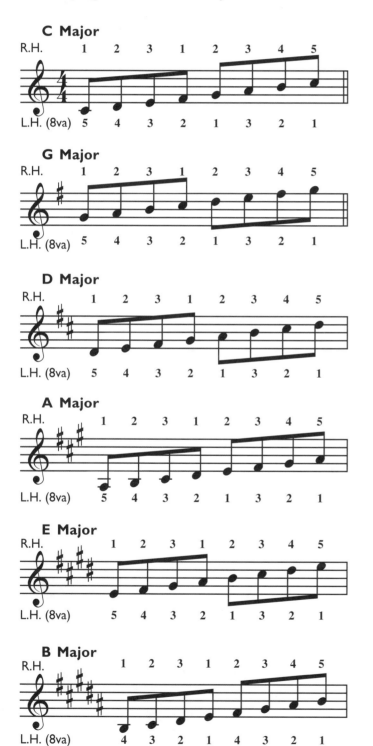

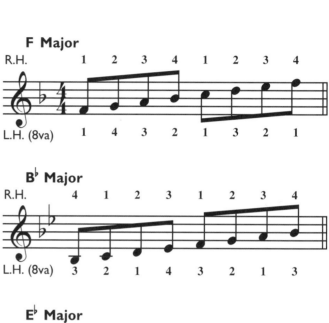